Teaching by Heart

Mimi Brodsky Chenfeld

Redleaf Press
St. Paul, Minnesota

Published by: Redleaf Press, a division of Resources for Child Caring
                450 N. Syndicate, Suite 5, St. Paul, MN 55104

Distributed by: Gryphon House
                P.O. Box 207, Beltsville, MD 20704-0207

"Do Spiderwebs Ever Wake You Up?" originally appeared in *Young Children,* July 1995. Reprinted by permission from NAEYC.

"On Wednesdays I Can't" originally appeared in *Young Children,* November 1994. Reprinted by permission from NAEYC.

"Your Assistant Is Getting Her Diaper Changed" originally appeared in *Young Children,* September 1995. Reprinted by permission from NAEYC.

"Welcome to Lala's Land" originally appeared in *Young Children,* July 1996. Reprinted by permission from NAEYC.

"Let's Keep the 'L' Word" originally appeared in *Educational Leadership,* April 1998, vol. 55, no. 7. Reprinted by permission from ASCD.

"Snowball" originally appeared as "On Behalf of Children" in *Early Childhood Education Journal,* 2000, vol. 27, no. 4. Reprinted by permission from Kluwer Academic/Plenum Publishers.

"The Whole Truth about Hole Language" originally appeared in *Early Childhood Education Journal,* 1996, vol. 23, no. 3. Reprinted by permission from Kluwer Academic/Plenum Publishers.

"Get the Elephant Out of the Room" originally appeared in *Young Children,* November 2000. Reprinted by permission from NAEYC.

"Telling Time" originally appeared in *Kappan,* February 1997. Reprinted by permission from Phi Delta Kappa.

An earlier version of "Schools Children Run To" appeared in *Educational Leadership,* September 1998, vol. 46, no. 4. Reprinted by permission from ASCD.

Library of Congress Cataloging-in-Publication Data
Chenfeld, Mimi Brodsky.
    Teaching by heart / Mimi Brodsky Chenfeld.
    p.   cm.
ISBN 1-929610-12-2
    1. Preschool teaching—United States—Anecdotes. 2. Early childhood education—United States—Anecdotes. I Title.

LB1140.23 .C44 2001
372.1102—dc21

                                        2001041631

To my mom, Iris Kaplan.
To the memories of Joe Kaplan and
Rose and Charles Chenfeld.
To my children: Cliff and Chana,
Cara and Jim, Dan and Kristi.
To my grandchildren: Len, Callie, Dylan,
Chloe, Ryan, Noah, and Landen.
To my "anchor man," Howard.
To ALL of our children and
to everyone who
loves and cares
for them.

Acknowledgments

I've had the privilege and good fortune to travel forty-four states and a few countries, crossing land and sea to be with teachers and children. I have learned from each and all! My list of THANKS to colleagues, kids, family, friends, and neighbors could circle the planet! For Redleaf's dear sanity, let me cite just a few folks and reach out in love and appreciation to all those who shared wisdom and experiences with me along the way but who spelled their names FRIENDS.

The stories in this collection have been enriched by

Pnina and Shai Berk
Chloe Brodsky Chenfeld
Len, Dylan, and Noah
  Chenfeld
Marilyn Cohen
Michelle Devoll
Tammie Ezzo
Maggie, Caryn, and John
  Falvey
Umberto, Domenico, Vesna,
  and Giuseppe Mangano
Pam Goldsmith
Carol Highfield
Oren Hayon
Gabriella and Jo Koehn
Debbie Lamden
Dr. and Mrs. Richard
  Langenbach
Ben Lichtman
Sung-Lyul
Tracy McCarty
Jim McMahon

Karen Mughan
Linda Muzzo
Harrison and Tracy Napper
Linda O'Brien
Emitle Pitzer
Max Rappoport
Shelly Reed
Paul Robinson
Ann Robbins
Marlene Robbins
Ben, Louie, and Zaide Rosen
Sharon Sazdanoff
Jana Schelb
Barbara Selinger
Dan Shealey
Helen Speyer
Rose Stough
Greg Vogel
Callie and Ryan Wilbat
Abby Wormbrand
Mindie Zisser

Love and thanks to Barbara Topolosky, Taryn Terwilliger, Sherie Wack, and the entire staff of fabulous educators at the Leo Yassenoff Jewish Center, Columbus, Ohio. Thanks to Terry Anderson, Jeff Murray, Tim Katz, Jim Arter, and ALL the schools and teachers and kids in the Greater Columbus Arts Council's Artists-in-the-Schools program and Children of the Future. Thanks to Leslie Zak, former director, and Clarissa Boiarski, present director, and kids and artists of Days of Creation Arts for Kids, Columbus, Ohio. Thanks to Mary Rykowski, principal; Peggy Fawcett, secretary; Marlene Robbins, dance teacher; Jim McMahon; and the kids and fellow teachers at Indianola Alternative Elementary School, Columbus, Ohio, especially the kids who graced this book's cover: Kai Hall, Sam Hatch, Alicia Padgett, Tao Quan, and Desirea Strickland. Thanks, Allen Zak, for photography patience. Thanks, Alan Rubin, for trying to make me beautiful. To Bertha Campbell, for telling me the story by heart.

Thanks to my family (see dedication)—to my sister, Laura Walcher, who reads everything I write with sharp and loving eyes; to Marilyn Cohen, my sister-in-love, who personifies teaching by heart; to Mike and Joy, Herb, and Bob, for TLC; to Michael Joel Rosen, who dazzles me with his creative gifts; to the greater families: the Cohens, the Blooms, the Walchers, the O'Briens, the Selingers, the Falveys, the Gandals, the Newmans, the Rappoports, the Wilbats, the Chenfelds, and the Kaplans.

Eileen Nelson and her wonderful Redleaf Press staff are deeply appreciated: Alex Lodner, Ronna Hammer, Jesse Singer, Alyn Bedford, and Ellen Hawley.

To each and every person who has ever touched my life—thank you!

MIMI BRODSKY CHENFELD

Contents

Foreword

To read Mimi Brodsky Chenfeld is to feel again
those first stirrings that made you want to teach, to
see again freshly, all the ways you knew you could
change the world through teaching. Her writing will
remind you of the profound responsibilities and
blessings that combine in the word *teacher*.

We are lucky to have Mimi in our field. Her joy in
teaching gives heart to every teacher she meets, and
her passion for teaching inspires even the most discouraged teacher. For those who aren't feeling good
and strong about their work and their relationships
with kids, an encounter with Mimi makes the sky
bluer, children's smiles sweeter, and problems easier
to tackle.

These essays were selected to reawaken and
sustain our delight and purpose in teaching. The
nineteen essays confirm the best instincts of
teachers and support them in staying true to those

instincts. Mimi reminds us how important kindness is to learning. She once summed up a guiding principle of teaching this way: "Don't be mean to little kids, and don't let anyone else be mean to them either!" She reminds us that kids need love and empathy, especially when they are learning hard things.

This collection is divided into three sections, each focusing on an important aspect of teaching: the kids (The Heart of the Matter), the teachers (Heart to Heart), and good places for kids (Having Heart). But you are invited, and even encouraged, to dive in and read the essay that most appeals to you at the moment. Pick up the book and read any essay when you have a minute; you'll walk away with a rediscovered sense of purpose and a more centered perspective.

Relax and enjoy these essays, then say proudly, "I teach."

EILEEN NELSON
DIRECTOR
REDLEAF PRESS

Introduction

I visited with a former preschool teacher and director who is now the administrator of a very unexpected but generous state grant for early childhood programming. Her office was crammed with data and deadlines, statistics and budgets. The barrage of administrative demands inundated her. She confessed that, a few days before, she had felt emotionally and intellectually drained. Hurrying from the office, she had jumped into her car and driven to a nearby early childhood center to spend the morning with the children. For the next few hours, she watched their puppet shows, finger-painted, sang "The Eeensy Beensy Spider," listened to *Goldilocks and the Three Bears,* ate snacks, and helped a few kids tie their shoes. When the morning session ended, she felt her strength had been renewed, her resolve clarified. After receiving hugs and the gifts of pictures and letters in the sacred handwriting of young children, she returned to her mission with a clearer head and a new determination to hammer out the best programs for the state's children and teachers.

This collection of articles and essays is really the equivalent of leaving the pressures of assessment, testing, documentation, evaluation, curriculum demands, scores, and skills, and driving to the nearest early childhood program to be with the children and their teachers!

Most early childhood educators are much too busy and tired to write their stories, so one of my callings in life is to share their stories with you. In the midst of today's relentless criticism of education and teachers, it's easy to forget that there is an eye in the middle of the storm. It's easy to forget what teaching is all about anyway! In most of the headline news about education, we rarely even hear the word *children.* We hear the language of business: products, outcome, budget item. But when we forget that it's all about our children, we are truly lost!

This collection is packed with true stories of children who run to their adults, who affirm, respect, comfort, and celebrate with them. As you ride out of the storm of editorials, legislation (often misguided), and bureaucratic pressures, remember from time to time, to go back to the *real basics*—the excitement, adventure, and delight of being with our youngest

children. Remember that their daily agendas have
very little to do with our formalized, preset curricula
and materials. The children are on their own timelines
and learning schedules. Every day is a world unto
itself in the life of a child! Among my layers of collected children's works, I found this note:

"Mimi, you're the Queen of Fun!"

That title means more to me than president or
prime minister!

Every summer, I gather the year's notes and boxes
of stuff to share with the undergraduate, graduate,
and in-service education students who are crazy
enough to sign up for my "Arts Across the Curriculum" course at Otterbein College. The students
come together from across grade and subject areas to
explore the integral role of the arts in every component of the curriculum, every aspect of learning. We
meet five Thursdays for eight hours a day.

Each season, as I gather my thoughts for the new
class, I find the same reminders repeated on the
backs of envelopes and on the margins of letters.
The main figure is a heart with the word *connections*
inside of it. On the first day of the course, I tell the
students, "Remember the word *connections*. By the
end of our time together, you'll know how important
that word is."

Making connections is what it's all about! As we speed through this high-tech, Internet-driven, zippy e-mail, instant-replay time, we often don't communicate. We miss each other. We disconnect. College courses in deconstruction are the current craze. We like to rip the component pieces apart, separate and analyze them. Too often, we forget to put them back together, synthesize them, and appreciate the sum total of their essences. Making connections is about seeing relationships—the myriad links between children and children, children and adults, schools and communities, curriculum areas, environments, cultures, timelines. When we lose our connections to one another, we become alienated and lonely. One of the greatest gifts we can give our children is the knowledge that they are part of the great family of human beans—not baked beans or green beans— that they are not alone but entwined and connected always. As you read through these shared moments, be sure to remember the heart drawn around the word *connections*. Without that bond of affection, mutuality, encouragement, and compassion, connections are almost impossible.

Over the years, the Otterbein summer students have asked to bring guests to class. My only instructions are, "They *must* participate. *No* spectators!" Oh, my! We've welcomed such a variety of guests:

grandparents, neighbors, friends, initially morose
teenagers who turned into creative class leaders.
This past summer, among our guest participants, we
welcomed (on the same day) a six-week-old infant
and an eighteen-month-old toddler. These two wonderful students stayed for the entire eight hours!
During the many musical, movement, drama, and
visual arts activities, our infant bounced, kicked,
and smiled with wide-eyed attention. During the sit-
down-and-talk times, she fell into a peaceful sleep.
Our merry toddler joined us with total joy when we
sang, played, performed, cut, pasted, and painted.
When the action paused for summarization or discussion, she curled up in her toddler seat, munched
her Cheerios, drank from her sippy cup, and dozed.

Education is a moving experience. But in spite of
all the important data and excellent research we
have about developmentally appropriate practices,
multiple intelligences, and brain function, many of
our school systems, media pundits, and state guide-
lines advocate doing *the opposite* of what children
need. Play is downplayed. Direct, hands-on, active
learning is minimized. Too many of our young children are sitting more and moving less; listening to
adult instructions instead of initiating their own
learning explorations; focusing on skills and work-
books to ensure high test scores instead of building,
painting, improvising, storytelling, and singing;
deconstructing instead of connecting. Look at our

two young guests who fell asleep during the more passive, purely verbal learning, who, when the music stopped and the movement stilled, munched Cheerios, drank from a sippy cup, and dozed. Before you read these stories, please fill a sippy cup with your favorite beverage, then take a well-deserved break when the reading gets boring! I'll forgive you if you doze off. We all have to understand when our students tune us out because we forget (or ignore) the best ways we all learn!

Last year, my great-niece, Maggie, now three and a half, was shy and unsocial in her playschool program. Her parents were concerned about her reluctance to participate. As I write this introduction, the telephone rings. Maggie's mom excitedly reports, "Maggie is *so* thrilled with school! Every day she comes home with her clothes covered with paint, mud, grass, and chocolate snacks! No clinging, no tears. She's exhausted, filthy, and happy!"

My deepest wish is that all of our children come home with the proud markings of a busy, active, meaningful day—with mud, grass, paint, and chocolate decorating their clothes and smiles on their faces. May their ecstatic families report that the kids are "exhausted, filthy, and happy!"

The Heart
of the Matter

Kids!

Do Spiderwebs Ever Wake You Up?

Oh, the Wonder of It All!

People who do not walk around with their sweater sleeves pulled out of shape by small, fingerpainted, sweaty hands; who do not have smudge marks on their faces from kisses pressed by tiny lips smeared with colored markers; who do not cut up their companions' food into bite-sized portions at gala dinner parties; who do not go on trips and shout, "Look, everyone! Cows! How many cows do you see?"; whose efficiently structured daily lives are filled with mature conversations and activities often ask me, "Why do you hang out with young children?" Sometimes I flip them an answer like, "Because they're there." Sometimes I shrug and give an answer like, "Just lucky, I guess." Sometimes I laugh. "Darned if I know," I say.

But I really do know. I hang out with young people because *I have to!*

In this shook-up, fast-lane, topsy-turvy, high-tech whirl of a world, where cool is hot and yes is no, where violence is epidemic and the lessons of history aren't learned, being with young children is like aerobics for the imagination, nourishment for the spirit. Sharing time with young children is like a splash in a deliciously cold, energizing lake on a smoggy, muggy day. The honesty of young children is startling.

In this fast-lane, topsy-turvy, high-tech whirl of a world, being with young children is like aerobics for the imagination, nourishment for the spirit.

My friend, six-year-old Maria, looked at my naked face with her clear eyes and asked, "Mimi, why are you so old?" Before I could answer, she took my hand and in a worried voice said, "I hope you don't die."

Being with children is a matter of life and death! It takes courage to spend time with young children. It takes a tough skin and a mushy heart. Young children keep me honest and brave.

In this crazy world of stereotyped thinking, of mass-media images and trite phrases, young children demonstrate originality as they share their love affair with language, with life.

When Brian announced that he had lost his first tooth, I asked him what he did with it.

"Put it under my pillow."

"What did you get?"

"I got a dollar!"

"Who gave you the dollar?" I asked.

"The Truth Fairy!"

Solving problems inventively in their expanding worlds is native to young children.

Jackie, another first-tooth loser, was excited as she told me about how her tooth fell out.

"Did you hide it under your pillow?" I asked in the familiar litany.

Jackie's voice dropped to barely a whisper, "No." she confided.

"Oh, why not, honey?"

"I didn't want the Tooth Fairy to come into my room..."

"So, what did you do?"

"I put my tooth on the top step of the stairs."

"Did the Tooth Fairy leave you anything?"

"Yes!" she exclaimed happily. "She left a quarter on the step!"

Young children remind us that the world is new and belongs to them. They own the moon, the sun, the stars, the songs.

Grandpa Joe was singing "Old MacDonald" to his two-year-old friend, Pnina.

"No, Grandpa Joe. No!" Pnina tried to shush him.

Grandpa Joe stopped singing. Pnina wagged her finger at him.

"No! Grandpa Joe, Pnina's 'Old MacDonald Had a Farm!' My song!"

Why do I hang out with young children? Because being with young children is a lesson in loving. In our statistical society, where feelings are hoarded, measured, metered, splintered, we learn about wholeness.

Four-year-old Oren's mom watched in shock from the kitchen window as Oren picked every flower in the garden. He ran to the back door, presenting his treasure to her.

"These are for you, Mommy."

"Oren, one flower would have been enough for me. You didn't have to pick all the flowers!"

"No, Mommy," the little boy explained. "I love you too much for just one flower. I love you more than all the flowers!"

Young children keep us from getting stuck in neutral. They make us drive in the center lane of life.

With young children, we are always connected to amazement. They faze us!

I was sitting with a few young children around a library table, talking about their favorite kinds of clothing. I was taking notes because these were interviews for my textbook, then in progress.

As they shared their opinions about styles and colors, they moved closer to me. The smallest child settled in my lap. My pen scribbled along with their conversation about Sunday clothes, sandals, blue jeans, Mickey Mouse T-shirts. In the midst of the lively exchange, five-year-old Aleah looked at me with wide eyes and asked, "Mimi, do spiderwebs ever wake you up?"

I spend time with young children so that I can be continually astonished. Their observations delight and inspire me. Their questions challenge me to face my own immense ignorance.

I spend time with young children so that I can be continually astonished. Their observations delight and inspire me.

When I'm with young children, I wish on Twinkle Twinkle Little Star, I clap for Tinkerbell, I cry for Charlotte, I brake for beauty, I notice a single ant climbing a blade of grass, I grow toward the light.

The magical wisdom of young children is contagious.

I was explaining to the three- and four-year-olds on the last day of preschool that my little dog puppet, Snowball, was going to Peek-a-Boo Summer Camp so he could keep practicing the peek-a-boo trick because he couldn't ever get it right. Some of the children smiled and said, "We're going to camp too." A few just looked and nodded. The older, more sophisticated four-year-olds watched me with X-ray eyes.

Know-it-all Brett challenged me: "He's *really* a puppet, isn't he?"

"Yes, of course he is."

Brett pondered for a few seconds, then came over and kissed the little peek-a-boo student. "Have a good time in camp, Snowball!"

Why do I hang out with young children? Because in all my years, no one had ever before asked me the answer-defying question, "Do spiderwebs ever wake you up?"

(And, how are we helping our children keep the wonder?)

On
Wednesdays
I Can't

Last Wednesday was my day with kindergartners at a nearby school. Oh, what fun to play around with nursery rhymes, Shel Silverstein poems, Winnie-the-Pooh characters, and baby animals in the oldest and most joyful of ways—song, dance, story, laughter, and improvisation. After our bouncy, active session, the children in the last group were getting ready to return to their classroom and continue exploring their ideas in words and pictures.

Because many of the children were barefoot (I always invite my friends to take off their shoes and socks if they want to, but I tell them they don't have to), the floor was strewn with kids pulling on socks, lacing or fastening their running shoes, snapping their sandal straps. Jimmy walked over to me and asked, "Mimi, could you help me tie my shoes?"

"Sure."

As I bent down to accommodate the request, I heard his voice from above, explaining matter-of-factly, "Some days I can. Some days I can't."

That seemed like a very clear message. I responded, "Me too. Some days I can and some days I can't."

His shoes tied, I stood up. Jimmy looked at me with calm, confident eyes, and before he turned to go, he announced, "On Wednesdays I can't."

As the children waved and hugged good-bye, I slapped Jimmy an extra high five. Thank you, Jimmy, for reminding me of what I sometimes remember and sometimes forget. Michelangelo (not the turtle) had a wonderful moto: "I am still learning." Jimmy, thanks for reinforcing that idea.

Sometimes we can and sometimes we can't. My neighbor the walker walked three miles on Monday. Today, he admitted, he only walked two. Maybe he didn't sleep well. Maybe it was the humidity.

Howard usually swims his laps in half an hour. Sometimes it takes him longer. On super days, he slashes through the water in twenty-five minutes.

Cara's handwriting is calligraphy. Once in a while, she scribble-scrabbles a note. "Just lazy," she explains.

Len the muffin man is potty trained. Mostly.

Baby brother Dylan sits up by himself. Usually.

Almost always, Callie Callie Coo pronounces her

new words clearly. Sometimes she needs an inter-
preter.

But I think Jimmy had an additional message:
I resist narrow, limited definitions. Don't stuff
me neatly into learning-style systems. Don't think
I'm totally predictable. Don't file us humans away
in computer disks—we're full of surprises!

Catch us on a good day and one, two, three,
we're awake! Alert! Everything comes together.
We're a symphony of synthesis. Test us then. We'll
score!

But don't test us on Wednesdays. On
Wednesdays we can't.

Your Assistant Is Getting Her Diaper Changed

A Call for Help

Pnina and I have a date at eleven to plant a garden
in her backyard. Before I leave to meet her, I call
ahead to verify our plans. No answer. I try her downstairs neighbor, Bubbe Iris, who reports, "Your assistant is getting her diaper changed!"

Eleven o'clock. Two-year-old Pnina, smelling
sweet as spring, joins me, carrying her pail, shovel,
and a little watering can. For the next hour, we clear
our land, breaking up clumps of dirt, scooping out
holes with our trowels, choosing the order and
design of our colorful annuals, smoothing over the
newly dug beds, and watering. Pnina is more than an
assistant—she is a colleague!

Even two-year-old people who need their diapers
changed want to help! In addition to helping in the
garden, Pnina picks up toys, carries boxes, delivers
mail, sorts clothes, and adds soap to the washing

machine. Her older friend Len, two and a half, proclaims daily, "I want to help!" And he does: he carries, loads, packs, sets, sponges, mixes, fixes. Be sure to include him in the chore of the moment. He's ready, able, and willing.

At age six, Harrison loves to wash mirrors, scrub toilets, cook soup, scramble eggs, spray-shine his favorite leather chair, and vacuum the floor. His mom, Tracy, knows he won't do it perfectly. But, she explains, "I'd rather have a kid who is learning to work with others, to pitch in, to know he's needed, to be responsible, than have a child who's afraid to try because he isn't perfect!" We do ourselves and our children a great disservice when we don't include them in family and household responsibilities.

> *I'd rather have a kid who is learning to work with others, to pitch in, to know he's needed, to be responsible, than have a child who's afraid to try because he isn't perfect!*

Watch children at play. They practice work! They set tables with dishes and silverware, they cook real-looking fake food in miniature pots on tiny stoves. Their little lawn mowers follow behind big lawn mowers. Their shiny fire engines race to the rescue. Ben and Louis hammer and measure along with Grandpa Z (Zaide). Their tool chest is at your service. Len is making you a hamburger. Do you want ketchup?

Four-year-old Melissa informs her father that she is going to marry her preschool classmate Julian. Her dad retorts, "Marry Julian? How are you going to pay the rent or pay for food? Does Julian work? Does he have a job?"

At first Melissa is glum, but then she perks up. "He *does* have a job! He's the line leader!"

Caryn Falvey is preparing for her first teaching assignment, a third-grade class. She calls triumphantly to report that she's all ready for the first day of school. I don't want to burst her bubble. I want her to blow another bubble. I challenge her. "Caryn, do you have a helper chart or wheel?"

"I have a job board."

"How many jobs on it?"

"Oh, about ten."

"How many children in your class?"

"Twenty-four."

"How about twenty-four jobs on your job board so every single day every single child has an important contribution to make to the life of the group?"

Caryn rises to the occasion, and in a few days, a copy of her lengthy list of student job assignments arrives in the mail. Some of the jobs are assigned to two people. Here is a sampling, with a few descriptive notes:

- Closet Monitor (makes sure that our supply closet is neatly organized at the end of each day)
- Art Center (makes sure that the art center is clean and neatly organized at the end of each day)
- Supply Monitor (distributes supplies to students)
- News Reporter (reads the paper, watches TV, listens to the radio to prepare for reporting one news event to the class)

Other jobs include Clocks (schedules day's events), Floors, Lights, Messenger, Chalkboard, Plants, Writers' Workshop Monitor, and Journals Monitor.

Caryn succeeds in defining important jobs for every child to perform every day. Can you?

We humans are a social, interdependent, communicating species. We need each other. Don't we learn best when working and playing together in safe, loving, cooperative environments, where each person is valued and the contributions of all members of the group are respected?

As I make notes to develop this theme, time passes. We have a week of drought followed by a week of rain. Today the sun is shining. Our flowers are growing. My notes can wait. I have a date with Pnina. Just as soon as her diaper gets changed, we have to weed the garden!

Welcome to Lala's Land

We're at one of the human-made wonders of the world—The Annual Conference of the National Association for the Education of Young Children! Catch the event in D.C. with a wide-angle lens. Picture 25,000 people from fifty states and a dozen countries attending 1,000 workshops and countless parties, meetings, and exhibit booths.

Close in on the overflowing crowd jammed into and around room 40, hall C, upper level of the D.C. Convention Center, pushing to hear music makers Greg and Steve. Follow your lens through the crowded hallway until you focus on a tiny spot of calm in a corner of the corridor crush.

Welcome to Lala's land!

Cuddled on her mommy's lap, a finger's touch away from the security of her stoller, fifteen-month-old Gabriella, who calls herself Lala, is playing with an empty shopping bag, demonstrating (once again) that children's best gifts are the wrappings! Born in China, flown across the world to her new American mother, Lala listens to the rock-and-roll rhythms of Greg and Steve's music. She wiggles and wriggles and claps to the beat. Waving her arms, she leaves her mom's lap and dances. She sways. She bounces.

Cuddled on her mommy's lap, fifteen-month-old Gabriella, who calls herself Lala, is playing with an empty shopping bag, demonstrating (once again) that children's best gifts are the wrappings!

Across the busy hall, I am tapping to the music and watching Lala. I have heard that the custom in some cultures is for people to be together without speaking for a while, sensing each other, becoming aware of each other. I keep my distance, keeping a close eye on the dancing child. When she sees me moving to the music, she stops, looks, waits. I smile, clap my hands. She claps too, smiling. Suddenly she turns and runs back to the safety of her mommy's arms, the nearness of her stroller. The music throbs on. Her feet can't help but dance. Hands must clap the beat. Again and again, Lala leaves her safe nest to move closer to me. She almost comes to me. No, run run run back to her mom. She is a jumpy, hoppy little girl on a big

journey: the journey from the known to the
unknown; the adventure of a new experience.

Now she comes all the way, and we dance and
clap and laugh together. She takes my small maraca
and shakes it to the music. Hurry back to Mommy to
give her the instrument. Lala shares. She likes to
share her treasures with others. I take out my little
puppy dog puppet, Snowball. He waves to Lala.
Another journey from Mommy to Snowball for a hug,
a kiss, a dance together.

When the concert is over, doors swing open and
the crowd rushes out into the already crowded hall.
In the midst of the noise and confusion, Lala sits
safely and calmly on her mommy's lap, reading one
of her favorite books. She is capable of focusing, of
sustained interest, of paying attention. The numerous distractions don't distract her.

Later that night, I am hanging out with a wonderful group of teachers, presenting a workshop. What a
surprise to see Lala and her mommy! One, two, three
and Lala is on the stage. After a few moments of
blinking and settling, she recognizes her dancing
friend, her puppy dog puppet Snowball, and her
shake-'em-up rattling maraca. She hardly notices the
applauding, cheering crowd watching her as she
dances, kicks, claps, turns, smiles, laughs, and wiggles to the music we are playing.

If she could speak a language educators could understand, she would probably stop the music and ask, "What are you cheering for? What are you looking at? You should know what we do. I'm not doing anything unusual. This is what little kids do! (Boy, adults are weird.)"

From the soles of my feet to the soul of my heart, I am happy. Here is a hands-on, direct experience demonstrating the meaning of our workshop words. No handouts required! Everyone present knows that this fifteen-month-old toddler is the workshop. She should be the conference keynote! She is both the message and the messenger. She is the heart, the heartbeat of the conference. In the midst of 25,000 teachers attending 1,000 sessions, we remember, we discover and rediscover the gentle, loving, joyful celebration possible in Lala's land. No tickets necessary for the land of early childhood!

Max Explains It All

Sitting with five-year-old Max as he works the keyboard of his computer with nimble fingers, and watches the changing scenes on his screen with total attention, I dare to interrupt his game.

"Max, I have no idea what you're doing. I have no knowledge of this game. As you play, would you tell me what you're thinking, what you're doing, what's happening so I can understand it?"

Without taking his eyes from the action, he nods. He talks. I ask questions and write.

"Where are you now?"

"World Two. I fell in the crack. I just died. I just died again."

"What's that?"

"That's a mushroom. I jumped. Those guys are bad guys. Now I'm banging coins."

"Why?"

"To get points."

"What do points do?"

"I don't know. I just banged a beanstalk. It took me to a different world. Now I'm in World Eight.

"I'm getting more gold coins. I can get more points. Uh oh, more bad guys.

"I forgot to jump.

"I just died.

"I'm starting back at the end. I just jumped on him. He's dead.

"When you get the mushroom, you get bigger."

"What's in this world?"

"There's more cracks. You can die a lot.

"The star makes you invisible. You change back to your own self when the star goes.

"Now I'm going in the Second World here.

"After I beat those bad guys, there's gonna be another star.

"I just got littler.

"Oh, more gold coins.

"More bad guys.

"I can't get the star 'cause I can't get bricks.

"Here come two more bad guys. I got them. Here's two others.

"I got the gold coins.

"More bad guys. Eater plants.

"I'm coming out of a hole. I almost died, but I didn't.

"Another bad guy.

"I got a mushroom and now I'm bigger.

"Now I'm in World Four. It makes you run fast.

"I just jumped over a crack.

"I just got little from a bad guy.

"I got to the first castle.

"I just got littler so I can get the beanstalk. The beanstalk is good.

"I'm climbing up the beanstalk. I can go up and down and jump over it. Look at all the gold coins!

"Now I'm in World Eight-One. It has trees. More bad guys.

"I just died.

"I have three more turns.

"I just died again 'cause I forgot to jump over.

"Now I have two turns.

"I just died again.

"One more turn for me.

"I died again. Game over."

"Why do you like this?"

"It's fun. You can jump, run fast, walk, go down tubes, get more gold points.

"The points are good.

"I just got to the top of the flag and got 5,000!

"I got to save the princess. You'll never see me until I go back."

"How do you know those are bad guys?"

"'Cause Mom read the instructions."

"Explain the game to me again, please."

"This is called Nintendo.

"I got two hundred points already, and I jumped over cracks.

"This is Mario and his brother Luigi."

"Tell me about them."

"What Luigi does for a living is jumping, running, walking, saving, and killing."

"What are you doing now?"

"I missed a fire flower cane. I didn't want it.

"I jumped over bad guys. I almost killed a bad guy.

"I got to the castle. I'm getting more gold coins.

"The flagpole swings you around.

"Those clouds are bad because they drop spiny things.

"This is Five. There's bullets in here, but I can get past it.

"I almost got killed, but I was invisible 'cause of that star.

"After I die, that's it for me.

"Now I have to put it away 'cause that's the rule of the game."

"Well, how did you do in the game?"

"One world is one lifetime. So, I just had twenty lifetimes and I beat twenty worlds, so I'm pretty good.

"That's it."

We have milk and cookies. I'm ready for a walk, but Max isn't finished playing yet. I'm ready for small talk. I want to say, "That tree outside is so tall it must be pretty old, and what was that song you learned in kindergarten about a baby whale, and did you hear the riddle about the chicken crossing the road," but my friend isn't into small talk now. He's got larger issues on his mind, like saving the princess and getting into the castle. He's five years old and into his twentieth lifetime. I'm still working on my first! His vocabulary is amazing. I sit in awe at his high-tech, small and large motor coordination. The advanced concepts he comprehends and expresses confound me. What was I playing when I was five years old?

> Imagine Max coming to kindergarten. Imagine the teachers who wait for him. Are they prepared to challenge and stimulate these millennium children?

There's a lesson in here somewhere. Imagine Max coming to kindergarten. Imagine the teachers who wait for him. Are they prepared to challenge and stimulate these millennium children? Do they dare offer boring, passive learning experiences? Do they realize that they must engage Max's imagination, language ability, curiosity, active involvement, sense of adventure? Do they respect his knowledge?

They must try to distract him from the challenges he is facing on his computer—challenges teeming with life-and-death obstacles. They must remember that Max is readying himself for his next lifetime in the worlds that are waiting for him.

Are we ready for Max?

Heart
to Heart

Teachers!

As We Believe,
So We Teach

I am spending time with two kindergarten classes
this week in an Arts-in-the-Schools residency. The
theme in both classes is the circus, and both classes
are using the theme to learn many skills and facts.

Let's visit room A, a very neat and orderly place.
On the bulletin board, a large, colorful poster from
one of the resource centers features a shiny, smiling
circus clown. On the shelves are books about the
circus. The children are working quietly at their
tables, filling out worksheets about the circus. A
box of clown pictures is waiting for them. Those
who have finished their seatwork are waiting
patiently for the clown project. When everyone
is ready, the teacher will instruct them in making
the clown. After the worksheets are checked and
marked, they'll go into their circus folders, which
are already thick with dittos and papers.

Moving on to room B, we open the door to parade music. On the shelves are books about the circus. Colorful circus mobiles made by the children swing from a rainbow-colored clothesline. An assortment of child-made circus posters decorates the walls. The children's tables have been moved about. Some of the kids are cutting and coloring on their own. A few children are in the midst of joint projects—clay animals and acrobats. The room is abuzz with activity. What's all the excitement? Only two more days to the big top! The kids are making some of their props and costumes and using others that come already made: hula hoops, balloons, clown masks, wigs, tightropes. It takes a few minutes to find the teacher, who is sitting, head bent, intent on assisting the Monkey Group as it clarifies its third variation for its feature act.

On the nearby wall is a collection of circus words illustrated by cutouts and original drawings. Every day, the children add more words as they think of them.

We—the teachers—are the curriculum, not our letters home, not what we hear, not the sayings and slogans we hang on our walls. The curriculum is what's inside. As we believe, so we teach!

Both classes share the same curriculum. The same letter went home to all the kindergarten families announcing the theme. But what a difference!

What is the difference?

The difference is between the teachers. Room A's teacher has a different belief system than does her colleague in room B. She believes that learning is a highly structured, teacher-directed, tightly controlled program. Children need to follow directions closely. She doesn't believe in the value of individual decision making, the importance of music, the delight of movement, the challenge of group planning. She isn't comfortable with scribbly pictures and unwieldy walls of words. There's no reason for adding to her vocabulary list. She's happiest when her students are sitting quietly doing seatwork. When they get too wiggly, she'll often say, "If there's any more wiggling, no recess!" She is under pressure from families, the school system, and the state to ensure that her kindergartners are competently prepared for the life of tests and measurements in store for them, and this convinces her that she hasn't the time for all the "monkey business" going on next door. Once you let kids move about freely, you lose control. She's sure her class will go wild if she gives them permission to "be" a circus character.

For her class's culmination of the theme, the students will perform a little play about the circus that she found in a children's magazine. The parts have already been assigned. As soon as the children finish their clown pictures for the hall bulletin board, they'll rehearse the play. Those who don't have parts will be the audience. They'll wait while the others practice. Her students are used to waiting.

Both rooms have a circus theme. Will *circus* be the same for the children in room A and room B?

We—the teachers—are the curriculum, not our letters home, not what we hear, not the sayings and slogans we hang on our walls, not the titles and labels carved above our portals or the headlines pinned on our bulletin boards. The curriculum is what's inside. As we believe, so we teach!

And the children know. They can sniff out the truth more sensitively than dogs sniff out a suspicious stranger.

Some of my beliefs:

- I believe in music, one of our first languages and the language of the human spirit. Many of our babies sing before they speak.
- I believe in movement, our first sign of life. We worry when something stops moving for a long time. It's unhealthy to ask children to sit still for long periods of time.
- I believe in helping children make connections and see relationships.

- I believe in encouraging children to actively participate in their own learning process. Education is a journey with its own timeline, its own unfolding that is unique to each learner.
- I believe that the children who come to our sacred spaces must find challenges, successes, friendships, strengthening, and skills that are fun and taught with creativity, in holistic ways. This begins the love of learning that will last throughout their lives.
- I believe that if we don't love and honor children, we should consider another profession.
- I believe that I need to hurry to the kindergartners in room B. I promised the circus paraders that I would help them with their banner-waving, circus-dancing march.

It's dismissal time. Marilyn Cohen, a little more dressed up than usual in preparation for an early evening school program, holds hands with her friendship circle of kindergartners as they sing their good-bye song. When the last child leaves, waving a fistful of artwork, Marilyn hurries to check the incubator, which is on a table in the center of the room. It has been the center of attention for the last month. She tidies up the poems, projects, pamphlets, and posters (the four Ps!) that are scattered around the incubator. She places two of the children's most beloved books back on the shelf: Mildred Selsam's *Egg to Chick* and Ruth Heller's *Chickens Aren't the Only Ones.*

She checks the eggs again, then glances at the children's chick-hatching calendar, though she knows full well what it says. It says "Day 21," but not one of the eggs shows any sign of a chick.

Staring at the apparently lifeless eggs, Marilyn thinks of the weeks of effort put into this activity: observing, comparing, discussing, researching, anticipating. And all the fun: the stories, songs, games, and poems the children enjoyed as they waited for the chicks to magically start hatching—one, then another, and another. Child after child has asked, "They *will* hatch, won't they, Mrs. Cohen?" How could she face her students and tell them that their fears have been confirmed, that their loving care and dedication have yielded nothing, nada, zero, zilch!?

Disappointment often drives teachers to leave the profession. But Marilyn doesn't give in to disappointment. She rushes to the office telephone and dials the number of Dr. Richard Langenbach. Years ago, the embryologist/farmer visited her class and conducted an in-service presentation on chick hatching. Marilyn was among those enchanted by his wisdom and enthusiasm. Since then, Dr. Langenbach has supplied eggs to Marilyn and her kindergartners for their springtime chick-hatching celebration, and their success rate has been outstanding—until now. Dr. Langenbach answers the phone, and Marilyn is relieved to hear his voice.

"Do you have any chicks up your sleeve?" she jokes, then explains her predicament. "I'm not going to lie to the children," she assures him. "Tomorrow, we'll talk about nature and how sometimes things don't work out the way we plan, the way we hope. Sometimes, it's not in our hands. We do our best, but then nature has its own plan. It's hard to understand, but we have to accept that. However, I do want the children to have chicks tomorrow to see what their chicks would have looked like if they had hatched the way we hoped they would."

She arranges to borrow about half a dozen live chicks, cancels her immediate plans, and drives fifteen miles to Dr. Langenbach's farm out in the country. But he isn't there.

"He must have forgotten," says Mrs. Langenbach, explaining that her husband just left a few minutes ago. Marilyn, determined not to leave empty handed, asks if Mrs. Langenbach would round up some chicks for her.

"Oh, my! I'm allergic to all those chickens," Mrs. Langenbach says apologetically. "I never go back there! But you're welcome to if you'd like."

So Marilyn digs her high heels into the muddy earth and heads for the chicken coops. "I didn't see this in my job description," she muses. She is greeted by a cacophony from hundreds of clucking, flapping, squawking, agitated chickens.

Where are the chicks? As she searches, she recalls how Dr. Langenbach talked about the developmentally appropriate practice of integrating chicks into the adult population. She peeks into the coops, and the birds peck her and scratch her. She finds herself in a flurry of chicken coop dust, feathers, and empty seed husks.

Amid the cackling chaos, Marilyn manages to capture six chicks. She puts the frightened little creatures into a cardboard box she brought, then gladly accepts Mrs. Langenbach's offer of a washing facility. She drives back to her classroom and gets the chicks settled into their temporary homes.

Every day, in ways rarely noted, teachers of all subjects and grade levels, in every town and city of this country, demonstrate the meaning of love.

The next day, as her students arrive, they are thrilled to see the chicks. Marilyn explains to them where the chicks came from.

They all talk about life's disappointments and joys—of eggs that don't hatch and those that *do*.

All the students get to be photographed holding a chick. Their photos will always be reminders of this special time.

Some would call Marilyn's experience an example of professionalism. Others would say she was nuts. I offer it as an example of what the poet Theodore Roethke meant when he wrote, "Teaching is one of the few professions that permits love."

Every day, in ways rarely noted, teachers of all subjects and grade levels, in every town and city of this country, demonstrate the meaning of love. Marilyn Cohen is just one example. Here are some more:

- Rosie postpones the surgery she needs until the summer because she doesn't want to leave her third graders in the middle of the school year.
- Marcella rises at five A.M. on trash collection days and drives around the neighborhood to find discarded but perfectly good items she can use in instructional activities with her students.
- John turns down an invitation for a special breakfast program. The tall Texan explains that he just can't miss his Head Start class, where he greets every child at the door with his ritual of "Howdy, pardner! I'm mighty glad to see you!"
- Maddy holds an umbrella over her toddler construction workers for more than an hour to

shade them from the hot sun while they dig tunnels and roadways in the sand to create a storybook world.

- Rashid waits in line at the mall for two hours to get an autograph from a visiting sports celebrity for one of his eighth graders, who is a big fan.

- Maxine calls every one of her fifth graders' families to make sure they attend a poetry and art celebration at the local museum. She refuses to let any child miss out and spends the evening carpooling for those who have no rides.

- A newspaper headline reads "Teachers Buy Extras, Survey Says: More Than $400 Spent on Supplies." The article begins, "Whether for stickers, markers, a meal on a field trip, books, or even shoes, teachers say they regularly dip into their own pockets to help their students." Jeff knows all about that. He spends more than $1,000 a year for his fifth graders. He knows which ones can't afford lunch during field trips or bus fare for special outings, so he pays for them rather than see them excluded.

In our high-tech, ever more impersonal society, where we are often known more by our numbers than our names, it's reassuring to know that those special people teaching our children demonstrate the meaning of that trite, devalued "L" word—*love.*

There, I said it!

Oh, No! Not the "L" Word Again

Linda O. isn't climbing the walls today. She's climbing on her science table, reaching up to add a new number to the line of days that she and her children have been counting together. The number line is hanging on the wall above her science table. Now she's ready to climb down. While her first graders watch, their teacher sets one foot on the table and rests the other foot on the adjacent desk, which, unbeknownst to her, is set on wheels. The desk (with one of her legs precariously perched on top of it) begins to roll away from the science table (with her other leg precariously perched on *it*). In silent fascination, the children's eyes widen as they watch the table and desk go their separate ways. Linda O. is hanging in midair in an almost perfect split when the desk rolls totally away from the table, dumping her splat in the middle of the floor.

Although the pain is intense and she is convinced that this may be her last day on earth, Linda is a professional, a veteran teacher, so instead of crying out, calling 911, weeping and flailing in raw agony, she catches her breath and softly instructs her students to "please continue tracking along the story we were reading." The first graders bend obediently to the task, averting their eyes from their fallen teacher, who is still grounded in the middle of the floor and seeing stars. The only sound in the room is the studious turning of pages.

Linda O. is sweating profusely as the pain intensifies. She still can't move. From her splattered, semi-split position on the floor, she hears the trip-trap of little footsteps. One of her first graders is walking toward her, telling her something in a lispy voice.

"Mithus O, I brought you thum tithues [tissues]. I don't know why you're theweating [sweating]. You're not doing anything!"

Because this happens a few weeks before Thanksgiving (and you know what a busy and exciting time that is for first graders, what with history and environment and harvest and multicultural arts activities), Linda O. doesn't want to miss a day of school. Once she gets on her feet, she continues to teach. When school is out for the holiday, she drags her seriously injured leg through the building. Three weeks after her fall, she finally visits the doctor. After examining her leg and studying the X-rays, the doctor is amazed.

"Linda, you broke your leg! I have never seen anyone with a break like this still be able to get around!"

His amazement triples when he sees that her broken leg is healing itself.

Linda O. explains it this way: "He doesn't realize that I'm a first-grade teacher!"

Oh, no! It's that "L" word again! You won't find many illustrations of that word in newspaper headlines or TV features. Good news doesn't have the appeal of disaster in our violence-celebrating culture. But examples of the "L" word abound in schools and classrooms throughout the country. Yes, examples of that corny, overused, underused, mis-used, unmentionable, sorely needed word in action!

I once saw a poster that said, "The Best Way to Send an Idea Is to Wrap It Up in a Person." So let's look at a few more of the people who wrap up in themselves the idea of loving and caring about our children and making a difference in their lives. Most of them don't talk about the "L" word. They just do it, live it, *are* it!

Call it professional. Call it dedicated. Call it over-ly committed. Call it responsible. Let's just come right out and say it: love.

There, I've said it!

While presenting at a large conference, I'm told about the teacher's aide who spends time with early childhood special needs children and who, as a trained catheterizer, dispenses medical assistance with gentleness and caring. Voted the Outstanding Teacher's Aide in the state, he passes up the lunch-eon in his honor because he doesn't want the child who needs catheterization to feel uncomfortable with the stranger who would sub for him.

"First things first," he tells me.

Ms. Stough looks weird today! Why is she wear-ing eyeglasses that have been mended clumsily with masking tape? Why is her hair braided into queer pigtails and standing straight up in the air?

Most of the time, Ms. Stough's inner-city third graders get along just fine, feeling safe in the caring environment that is their classroom. But at other times, like today, the kids can be mean. One of Ms.

Stough's third graders has lice again. Everyone knows about it because her hair is swathed in petroleum jelly and tied straight up away from her scalp, in tight pigtails. The kids have been teasing her, so Ms. Stough tied her own hair into pigtails and stood with her arm around the little girl.

This same day, a boy's eyeglasses broke. Ms. Stough mended the frames with masking tape, and they did look clutzy and funny. Again, the teasing. Again, Ms. Stough to the rescue. She wound tape around her own unbroken glasses. The teasing stopped. The message is clear.

"I get kidded and razzed by the teachers and parents," Ms. Stough admits, "but those kids are safe."

Another example of the "L" word in action comes from a letter written by Barbara Selinger about her day substituting in a special education class of ten children from kindergarten through second grade. The children face daily emotional, physical, and behavioral challenges. Barbara puts in an exhausting day, and in the last few minutes, she sits down with a second grader who is quietly working alone. She asks if he needs help. He nods. His assignment is to pretend that it's the first day of school and write about what he had hoped school would be like and whether it is, in fact, what he hoped. The child has nothing to write. Barbara prods him with a few questions and receives minimal responses.

She asks him if he hoped to meet a new friend on the first day of school and he shrugs as he replies, "I don't have *any* friends. *Nobody* likes me and no one wants to be my friend."

Barbara says she disagrees with him, but they go on to write about a plain, ordinary day where nothing good happens. When he finishes, she asks him, "Can I tell you a secret?"

He nods.

She whispers in his ear that *today* he made a new friend.

He looks at her with big, questioning eyes.

Barbara asks, "Do you know who?"

"You?" he answers.

When Barbara says yes, the biggest grin brightens his face—a smile from ear to ear.

Barbara's letter ends with, "At that moment, I remembered why I became a teacher."

Admire the wall-to-wall ribbons of honor earned by boys who are court-assigned to the Riverview Juvenile Correctional Center. Troubled boys. Boys in trouble whose ages range from twelve to twenty. It's a tough place for the boys and for their teachers.

Six years ago, in spite of probably justified skepticism, science teacher Paul Robinson got an idea. Taking his students to a field outside the building, he inspired them with the possibility of a vegetable garden. It took hard, sweaty work to dig a new garden, but they did it. They planted many kinds of seeds—eggplant, pumpkin, squash. But the most important seeds Paul and the boys planted were seeds of confidence, self-esteem, responsibility, cooperation, community, patience, and caring for the earth. That first year, when Paul and the boys took their vegetables to the county fair, they won top prizes and honors. Since then, they have won many state and county awards. Now, with the assistance of his colleagues Jana Schelb and Dan Shealey, Paul and the boys have a colorful and bountiful garden blooming.

When I acknowledge the extra time, effort, and faith involved in this ongoing project, Paul simply says, "It makes science interesting, doesn't it?"

I wouldn't say it to this tough, dedicated educator, but I think it's—oh, no! It's the "L" word again!

To be continued—indefinitely.

Help! Just as Marilyn Cohen is gathering up photos, projects, books, and artwork to share with the community college students who will attend her conference presentation, she receives a call from the conference director asking her to please talk a little about her philosophy of and her beliefs about developmentally appropriate practices.

The assignment is more of a challenge for Marilyn than being with children! She has thirty-three years of rich and wonderful experience teaching kindergarten, but she is not a theory or strategy person. She's a hands-on, feet-on-the-floor, down-to-earth, child-oriented, playful, dedicated educator.

Now she's writing, revising, and rewriting some introductory notes. After a night spent tossing and turning and wrestling with her ideas, Marilyn types her introduction in bold type. (She has to type it out.

She is too anxious to wing it.) She plans to begin like this:

"You are likely to be overwhelmed by all the educational jargon and buzz words, like 'multiple intelligences,' 'program strategies,' 'curriculum planning,' 'emergent literacy,' 'whole languages,' 'proficiency testing,' 'accountability,' 'developmentally appropriate practices.' Oh, please, don't become discouraged, for I'm here to tell you that you are about to embark on a career that is fulfilling, rewarding, and sacred work. If you truly believe in the precious lives and spirits of the young children you teach, you and they will experience a joyful education journey, which will launch for them a lifetime of loving learning, and all those buzz words will fall comfortably into place."

I'm here to tell you that you are about to embark on a career that is fulfilling, rewarding, and sacred work.

Marilyn has spent most of her professional life doing. How should she put her beliefs into words? She struggles on:

"I constantly and genuinely modeled for the children a sense of wonder and amazement as I learned and discovered with them. I tried to create a stimulating and interesting learning environment and tried to take into account their interests and needs and developmental stages. I planned many opportunities for the children to explore, using all of their senses to discover their world. Children need to move, and their physical need to be actively involved must be considered...curriculum needs to be well planned, yet it is also vital to be extemporaneous and tuned into what the children are passionate about."

She is exhausted! She puts her notes aside and tries to decide what the workshop is really about. This leads her to mull over some of her most memorable times with kindergartners through the years. She focuses on three projects from her galaxy of sparkling examples. All three line up perfectly with principles of developmentally appropriate practices.

The first is her Runaway Gingerbread Boy Celebration, which she begins by reading the children one of the gingerbread boy books. After she reads the book, they make, bake, and decorate a big gingerbread boy cookie for the next day's snack. She and the children ask the custodian to keep the door to the kitchen closed so the gingerbread cookie doesn't run away after it's baked. After saying goodbye to the kids, she runs around the school planting gingerbread boy–shaped notes with clues that will take the kindergartners all through their new surroundings. The next day, she welcomes the kids and they go together to the kitchen for their gingerbread boy cookie and find the apologetic custodian handing them the first note, which says, "Ha, ha, ha/You can't find me/I'm the gingerbread boy/I ran to see/Where the children have lunch!"

She races through the school with the excited children, finding and following notes, discovering their new school, ending up in the principal's office, where he presents them with their gingerbread boy cookie. They fly to their own room to snack and talk and review the sequence of their journey. Then they write and illustrate an original book about their fantastic day and take turns bringing their book home to show to their families.

The second project is her Amazing Spring Chick Hatching. This involves the children in weeks of observing eggs, sketching, reading, comparing, measuring, researching, singing, and celebrating the arrival of the first newly hatched chicks.

The third is her Sunny Unit on the Sunflower, which spans weeks and includes exciting times of observing, appreciating, comparing, guesstimating seeds, counting (the children counted 1,750 seeds from their one sunflower this year!), measuring, and making sunflower snacks for children, gerbils, birds, and squirrels, not to mention planting, reading, painting, dancing.

Marilyn settles on the Runaway Gingerbread Boy Celebration and the Sunny Unit on the Sunflower. But she decides not to touch on the natural way the experiences line up with developmentally appropriate practices until after the conference participants rediscovered the children in themselves and joined her in telling about and having real experiences.

The community college students are enraptured by the stories.

Following the instructions of the conference's director, though, Marilyn must bring her session back to task on time. She asks the students to talk about how, in these two fun-filled experiences, the children's excitement, discovery, and adventures in learning harmonized with developmentally appropriate principles.

- Did the children learn with all their senses?
- Were the experiences interactive/hands-on/multi-curricular?
- Were they self-directed and open ended? Did they meet individual needs and provide for individual differences?
- Did they honor the multiple intelligences?
- Did the children have many opportunities to work and play cooperatively and try out their newly developing social and language skills?
- Did the children experience success?

And on and on down the list!

At the end of her session, Marilyn passed out gingerbread cookies and sunflower seeds.

In case Marilyn has any doubts how effective her approach to teaching really is, the school in which she taught kindergarten for the last twenty-eight years planned a marvelous party for her retirement. Two hundred and fifty people, from all places and of all ages, have sent in reservations. When I see the beautifully designed tables, set with sunflower centerpieces and tiny, decorative chicks, my tears flow.

When the committee displays books, pictures, murals, and letters to and about Marilyn from her current kindergartners and from alumni who graduated from her classes as long as twenty-eight years ago, tears gush!

One dad tells of taking a walk with his kindergartner. A barking dog stopped them. The child looked up at his dad and said, "I wish Mrs. Cohen was here now."

"Why?"

"Because she understands what animals are saying."

Another alumnus remembers that he was held back in kindergarten mostly because his motor skills were slow in developing. Instead of letting him feel humiliated and embarrassed, Marilyn told him that every year she picked a very special child to help her out with the new kindergartners. She said he had been chosen for that very important task! He had a wonderful second year in kindergarten. Now he had a chance to thank Marilyn and inform her that he is a successful surgeon!

Every single child in the school writes Marilyn a letter. I am most touched by the messages from her former kindergartners who are in the fourth, fifth, sixth, seventh, and eighth grades.

What do they remember of kindergarten? What do they choose to say in their colorful, illustrated letters to Marilyn? Just from enjoying these few excerpts, I think you will discover what is important to children, what they learn *by heart,* what they will cherish forever from their earliest school years. (Remember, the authors of developmentally appropriate practices didn't make up those principles. Children dictated them and the authors just wrote them down.)

- "I learned about magnets. I remember the chick book we made and I still have it. I have the picture of me holding the black chick with the broken leg. I remember how happy it made me feel when the chicks started to hatch. I remember when we grew the sunflower and ate the seeds. I remember eating the coconut and drinking the milk. I remember how much I loved the rabbit we had and the little jobs we had. I remember how kind, wonderful and caring and how great of a teacher you were. I love you and will miss you a ton when you leave."

SARAH G.

- "I especially liked when we had the caterpillars and watched them turn into butterflies. Then we went out to the playground and let them go. They were so beautiful. I think kindergarten was my first step toward the real world and I still dream that I'll get a good education and you're the one who inspired me."

  LAUREN S.

- "I had the best time! I remember so many things like when we made lemon lollipops for Mr. L. and applesauce after going to an apple orchard. Hatching chicks was fun. I always used to like to see if there were any cracks in the eggs in the morning, every day. When you took pictures of us, you gave us a memory of the hatching process. I still have mine."

  LASURIE M.

- "Kindergarten: happy, chicks, imagination, red circle, butterflies, letter people, rabbit, apple orchard, Star of the Week, gingerbread man, dinosaurs, fun."   RAFAEL C.

- "When I saw the letter tape I knew I was having fun, but what I didn't know was that I was learning. That was the fact with everything you had us do."   JOSH C.

- "I remember the gingerbread man and how we had to find it, the letter guys, I loved the butterflies and the chicks. Oh, yeah, the dress-up corner was so much fun. The dinosaurs were so cool. The five senses were some of my favorite things we did in kindergarten."

  JONI S.

- "Mrs. Cohen taught me how to be a nice class-mate."   NATARIA G.
- "Mrs. Cohen taught me the basics of every-thing except for friendship, which she taught me everything in."   JOSEPH T.

After a whole page of memories of chicks, butterflies, gingerbread boy hunts, sunflowers, and rainbows, Lilith B. ends her letter with:

"I remember your great teaching. I remember kindergarten.

"I remember

"I remember

"I remember."

(And what will *your* students remember from their sacred time with *you?*)

Before the party, Marilyn was asked to write something about her philosophy. She wrote it all in a three-line poem:

> *Amazed by chicks in spring,*
> *lured by sunflowers in fall,*
> *love of learning, best of all*

I have had it printed on a sky-blue T-shirt with a golden sunflower design. My gift to her was a nest puppet with hatching chicks. Through her years, she has helped hatch many a new, miraculous chick!

Marilyn Cohen recently retired from teaching after twenty-eight years in the kindergarten program of Bet Shraga Hebrew Academy in the Capital District of New York state.

No Rx for
Reading

O Reading! Our country is in a quandary about the best way (note the singular *way* instead of plural *ways*) to teach reading to our children.

We are so frustrated, so polarized. Remember, we are a fast-food, instant-gratification, high-speed, high-tech culture. We're into product, not process. We demand outcomes and inputs. We want more bang for our bucks! One size fits all! A newspaper headline reads, "Rx for better readers." Rx means prescription. Prescription means written order, rule, official law or direction. Prescription means recipe, cure-all, heal-all, command, formula, ordinance. Let me tell you about some friends of mine.

Rose

After thirty years of teaching the early grades in public schools, Rose plunged into a daring new adventure—learning Korean! Why? Her network of

new, caring Korean friends encouraged her to learn
their language so she'd be able to communicate
more easily with them and so she'd be prepared
when she visited South Korea. Bravely, Rose enrolled
at Ohio State University, taking Korean 101.

Her first lesson was that she was not an auditory
learner! Her Korean instructor was used to having
forty to fifty students in his classes back home, and
he taught in traditional ways—lecture, text, memo-
rization. Some of Rose's classmates (especially those
with some prior knowledge of the language) had few
problems following along. Others had difficulties.
Rose had great difficulties. She was ready to throw in
the towel! Urged to keep a journal of this new, challenging experience (Rose had other descriptive
words for this immense undertaking), she jotted
notes throughout this unprecedented, traumatic
quarter.

"I think in different ways. The text is no help at
all! I'm walking in like a young child who doesn't yet
know the symbols for the different sounds. I feel so
stupid! Like quitting. The instructor has no idea of
how some of us are struggling. I'm reading letter by
letter—the way a lot of kids do. When he tells us a
word, I have no carryover that those letters make up
that word."

Coming to her rescue, Rose's friends dedicated
their time and creativity to help her make sense out
of the unfamiliar symbols and sounds. Rushing out
for fast-food suppers, Rose's best friend, Sung-Lyul,

shaped Korean letters out of french fries. Throughout
those first weeks, her friends made letters out of
their fingers, drew story maps to clarify meanings,
used dramatically exaggerated gestures and voices
to help her comprehension, improvised songs that
helped her vocabulary.

"I definitely would have dropped the class if not
for Sung-Lyul and my friends coming to the rescue,"
she wrote. "Just like Home Support! Now I understand why so many children give up when they're
having difficulties and no one at home is there for
them. But kids can't drop the course. They drop
their spirit and just sit there not learning."

As the quarter went on, Rose learned a lot, but
she also helped her instructor learn. He slowed
down, made more time for questions, encouraged
more, loosened up.

"When I read the new word today, my instructor
said, 'Good!' It meant so much to me and I remembered my years of teaching children and thought
how important it is to keep in mind those little
(immense?) accomplishments and take time to celebrate them. Those moments motivate the learner to
continue with the struggle."

It took over a month for Rose to crack the code
of the three basic vowel symbols.

"I cried. I felt frustrated. Here I am, a teacher, trying to find techniques to help myself. I'm as frustrated as that little first grader, and I'm armed with ways
of learning!"

Thanks to french fries, fingers, drama, improvised songs, and a more flexible teacher, Rose is now reading simple Korean stories and menus. She can have brief conversations with Korean friends (if they speak slowly), can recognize more words than she can say, and feels very proud of herself but also deeply humbled:

"I wish I'd had this experience before I taught my thirty years of children. I would have been much more empathetic—more aware of the different ways children learn, the different ways we all learn. This experience gave me deeper insight into that complicated process called learning."

Umberto and Domenico

Vesna explains her family this way: "We are parents from two different cultures living in a third culture with our children getting educated in a fourth culture!"

Her children, Umberto (three and a half) and Domenico (two-ish), wave a cheery goodbye to Vesna as they run to their teachers at the Jewish Center's early childhood program. The two brothers speak and understand Macedonian, which they learned from their mother and her family. With their dad, Giuseppe, they speak Italian. English is the language they speak with their friends and their mom. In school, they are learning Hebrew songs and words. At very young ages, Umberto and Domenico are trilingual with a touch of a fourth language!

They love books. Story time is special time. Most
of the books Vesna reads to them are in English. The
boys know how books work—pages, left to right,
print and pictures moving the stories along. Almost
always, because they love their story time, they beg
Vesna, "Read it again, Mama" (and again, and again).

When their Uncle Chris returned home from a
trip to Macedonia, bringing children's books to his
nephews, the kids' grandparents read them the new
gifts. Sitting on their grandparents' laps, the boys
followed along in Macedonian, looking at the
Macedonian text. When the stories were over, the
boys begged in Macedonian, "Read it again, Dedo
[Grandpa]. Read it again, Baba [Grandma]!"

Whenever Vesna works at her desk at home, the
boys set up their desks and busily write their
reports and letters. They have a box filled with the
hieroglyphics of toddlers. When their Uncle Chris
was in Macedonia, Umberto concentrated on a very
special letter to him. He read the letter (written in
scribble-scrabble) to his mom:

"Dear Uncle Chris. I miss you very much."

Soon the boys' noodly letter shapes will magically transform into recognizable letters. The Roman
alphabet used by English and Italian will probably
emerge first, followed by the Cyrillic alphabet that
Macedonians use. Most certainly, the children will
recognize the designs of Hebrew letters from posters
and pictures in school. When mail arrives from their
Italian grandparents across the ocean, Umberto and

Domenico will have no trouble remembering to deliver those letters to their father, Giuseppe.

This is a hang-loose time in their lives and they are having the time of their lives! No one is pushing them, drilling them to learn the letters in any of their three languages. Their teachers, parents, and friends know that any minute Umberto will write a few words in English, Macedonian, or Italian when he writes another love letter to his Uncle Chris.

Ben

Please don't disturb Ben. He's finishing *The Phantom Toll Booth.* Ben is five years old.

Excuse me—five years old and reading *The Phantom Toll Booth?* How did this happen?

All we know is that Ben's family and babysitters have been reading to Ben since he was an infant. But haven't many of our children been read to since birth?

Ben was an early talker. At twenty months, he loved pointing to letters and words and delighted in naming the letters. His favorite words at one and a half were names of cars, which he identified by colors, styles, and even their owners: "That's a Mommy car—Volvo!"

When his mom bought a set of magnetic letters, he not only knew all of them but played jokes, taking out the M and replacing it with a W to trick people.

At two, he pointed out syllables and words on the pages of books that were read to him. He even read contractions correctly, saying "do not" instead of "don't." Riding in the car, he asked his mom, "What's 'one way'?" as they passed the road sign.

When he was two and a half, he was reading. If you handed him a Dr. Seuss book that he had never seen, he could read it.

At the zoo with his Aunt Marlene, Ben read the signs giving information about the animals. He was just three years old.

How Ben learned to read is still a mystery. Scientists don't know exactly how children like Ben make sense out of the symbols that form words and make meanings. Meanwhile, millions of parents and teachers are reading books trying to figure out how to help their children learn to read.

O Reading! There is no Rx for teaching you. We don't even have to teach children like Ben. These mystery children sit in their toddler seats in the back of your car and ask you, "What does 'one way' mean?" As you almost steer off the road, you realize that your two-year-old has learned to decode the language all by himself, without any conscious help from you!

Children who learn like Rose need french fries and fingers, songs and games, maps and pictures, clay, sand, and blocks to help them along on this incredible adventure.

Umberto and Domenico are good listeners. They learn easily, quickly, from tuning into the sounds and music and rhythms of words and language. Gestures, facial expressions, and movement patterns help them on this wondrous journey.

Our children celebrate the multiple intelligences of the human family. They learn to read by a combination of many print-surrounded, print-immersed experiences: from puppets to posters, from creative movement to field trips, from storytellers to story-telling to story writing to story reading. We learn in so many different ways, on so many different levels. Learning is a multi-dimensional, continuous, ever-evolving experience. No one Rx (no matter what its value) succeeds with all children.

We do know a few things. Children need to be welcomed into the world of language at birth. They need to be talked to, sung to, read to, included in the richness of language from infancy on. Children who grow up in lonely environments, with minimum inter-action and communication, who rarely see examples of print, who don't get lulled to sleep with lullabies and dazzled by stories, who have no one to walk along or talk along with them, will have problems learning how to read. They, as do all of our children, desperately need exciting, joyful, fun-filled early childhood programs rich in loving, dynamic learning moments and methods.

Get out the french fries and spell No Rx for Better Readers.

Having
Heart

Good Places
for Kids!

Proficiency Tests Are Robbing Our Kids

To an unprecedented extent, today's schools are relying on standardized, formalized tests. Whether the intention of those who have pushed for the wide-spread use of proficiency testing was to determine curriculum, bully teachers and administrators, and cause anxiety in children and families, I can't say. But here's the reality: This focus on a single score to evaluate our children's achievements, teachers' successes, and schools' goals has caused a grim limiting of quality, developmentally appropriate educational experiences for all students and a narrowing of opportunities for teachers to enrich the lives of their students with exciting, inspirational, and challenging materials and methods. And the proficiency-test virus has affected all age and grade levels.

Research shows that young children learn best in active, exploratory ways—through play, music, clay, sand, blocks, movement, painting, discovering. These are the oldest and most basic ways young children make meaning out of their world. But because of the tremendous pressure on all grade levels, our kindergarten children are now doing seat-work, worksheets, and formalized sit-down skills lessons. Play is downplayed. Joy becomes nothing more than a dishwashing liquid.

Many kindergarten teachers are expressing grief and anger at the pressure on their youngest students to read by the end of kindergarten, whether they are ready to or not. Why are these children (and their teachers) under such pressure? Because of fourth-grade proficiency tests.

The mother of a fourth grader called me to report, "It's only the first week of school. My child doesn't even know his teacher's name or all of his classmates' names yet, but he's already brought home two proficiency-test practice packets."

And what are our children learning from this? Mostly, how to take tests. Those kids who are already good test takers will do fine. But many people learn in other ways. Taking standardized, impersonal tests is not the way they show what they know. When a test is the only measurement of a student's abilities and achievements, many children are doomed to failure (and now Ohio has come up with a very questionable plan—to hold back thousands of fourth graders who do not meet the standard that the legislature has deemed minimal).

Do proficiency tests help children to become life-long learners? Creative, thoughtful problem solvers? Inquisitive, appreciative children of wonder? Take wonder out of learning and we have a packaged bread! Do proficiency tests inspire children to fall in love with reading and the exciting worlds that real learning helps them discover? Do these tests measure the learnings derived from unique and meaningful classroom experiences, or are they detached lists of often irrelevant questions that many intelligent adults find difficult to answer?

There are other ways to evaluate our children's learning. A few examples: portfolios, everyday assessments, reading records, anecdotal journals, performance and product evaluations. We humans have many different and valid ways to demonstrate that we understand information. Proficiency tests are only one very limited way.

Let's spend the vast amounts of money we are giving to proficiency testing on tutors, mentors, early intervention teachers, smaller classes, and enriched experiences such as field trips (many of which have been drastically cut because they take time away from controversial reading programs that prepare our children to take that proficiency test). Let's not diminish the ways we view our children, their teachers, and the endless possibilities of in-depth, compelling learning experiences. The spirits of our children, our teachers, and our administrators are endangered species.

A Year
in the
Land of Oz

When three-and-a-half-year-old Abby skipped merrily into Tammie and Greg's class one morning wearing her ruby red slippers, the room turned Technicolor! Glenda floated down in a bubble, waving her shiny magic wand. Toto barked. The Cowardly Lion roared. The whole class went mad for the Wizard of Oz!

Always alert and responsive, Greg and Tammie immediately dug up the musical score to the *Wizard of Oz* and played it. It was still early in the school year, but from that day until school ended in June, Abby and her classmates stayed on the Yellow Brick Road.

Tammie keeps notes on her children's interests and activities. Here is a small sampling from her journal, written as the days, weeks, and months went by:

- We've added witches' hats, funnels, and scarecrow hats to the dramatic play clothes. There's a white gown they use to be Glenda.
- Abby wears her ruby shoes to school. It's not uncommon for her to trade shoes with every girl throughout the day. We often have to switch their shoes while they're sleeping so we know they're going home in their own shoes.
- We had a dress-up day and Abby brought in her Toto, Lion, and Wicked Witch. She even had a Dorothy dress.
- A lot of the kids went to see Oz on Ice.
- When we watched the movie for the first time, the kids wore witch hats to ward off evil.
- When the children watch the movie, they'll get up and role-play the story in the scary parts.
- We have pictures and postcards with scenes from the movie hanging like mobiles.
- On sharing day, the kids bring in Oz books. They even brought in a song book from the *Wizard of Oz.*
- We are decorating the room. We'll have Oz and the Yellow Brick Road with grass, sky, sun, rainbow, ruby slippers. We'll create the Emerald City and the hot air balloon.
- We made a big Oz book.

- The children divided up areas of the room where certain acts in the story happen: the witch's castle; where they find the Tin Man, Scarecrow, and Lion; etc.
- Jacob made the connection between the Lion, Scarecrow, and Tin Man and the working farm-hands introduced at the beginning of the story. He even knew the workers' names.
- We've been talking about the brain, about the heart, and why we need them. We had a big discussion about not only the physical body parts but the emotional reasons why we need a brain and a heart. We talked about courage and tried to define it. The children shared a lot of examples from their lives.
- The kids sing the songs constantly and know almost all the words.
- We've made tornado bottles. We set up a town with Monopoly-game houses and spin the tornado through the town. We talked about weather and storms and the uniqueness of tornadoes.
- We're going to paint small witches' brooms green.
- We've discussed whether the Wicked Witch is green all over. The kids decided that she is green all over, even her belly button, and no, it doesn't wash off.

- We made Scarecrow, Tin Man, and Lion shapes.
- We talked about rust and oil and why oil is needed in rusty metals.
- We wondered why the colors change after Dorothy goes over the rainbow. We read about and discussed colors and rainbows.
- We've watched the movie three times, munching the popcorn we made.

Greg and Tammie saw the kids every day. I spent time with them once a week, connecting curriculum areas to movement, dance, and music experiences. ("We have removement with Mim!") Over the years, I have danced with children to and about topics from magnets to planets, from time to rhyme, from one to one hundred, and from A to Z. You name it and we've turned it into moving moments.

When Tammie and Greg's kids first fell in love with Abby's red slippers, I didn't think twice about making a connection between the curriculum themes and concepts the teachers wanted to highlight and the Wizard of Oz images. After all, we needed loose, floppy movement for the Scarecrow; tight, rigid movement for the Tin Man; big, brave, but then small, shy movement for the Lion. The story lends itself perfectly to movement exploration, which of course enriches vocabulary, comprehension, and imagination.

As long as we began our sessions with the children turning into their favorite characters as they crawled, skipped, slipped into our dance room; as long as we spun around like whirling tornado winds; as long as we flopped dramatically on the floor like the doomed house the storm dumped on top of the wicked witch; as long as we marched joyfully singing, "Ding dong the witch is dead!" in our parade of cheering Munchkins; as long as we flew around the room like flying monkeys; as long as we could decide whether we wanted to be the characters throwing water on the W. W. of the W. (Wicked Witch of the West—we soon reduced the important elements to intials) or be the witch melting, we could interlace with any curriculum area on any teacher's wish list!

The story lends itself perfectly to movement exploration, which of course enriches vocabulary, comprehension, and imagination.

Dorothy and her friends celebrated Thankgiving, Hanukkah, Dr. Martin Luther King Jr.'s birthday, snow, trees, the circus, the Three Pigs, and Peter Pan! As long as we didn't stray from the Y.B.R. (Yellow Brick Road), we could learn about everything!

By now, the families of the children were growing concerned about this fascination with the W. of O. A meeting was called, and this issue was central.

"What the heck is going on already?" bewildered family members asked.

Tammie explained, giving a chronology of the class's obsession, starting with the fateful day Abby danced into class with her ruby red shoes. I threw in my ten cents and told the befuddled audience that I usually hid the W. of O. album (yes, friends, I must confess: I prefer my old records and historic phonograph!) deep in my pile of records. But in a fraction of a second, the children *always* found that record, waving it in the air like a victory flag. I reminisced about how, after winter break, the children rushed to me, shouting, "Mimi! Don't forget! You promised us the Lizard of Oz!"

A few parents were inspired to come and observe our movement sessions. The next day, I greeted the visitors as the children crawled, flew, and skipped into the room announcing which characters they had chosen for the day.

As long as we didn't stray from the Yellow Brick Road, we could learn about everything!

"I'm Dorothy!"

"Me too!"

"I'll be Toto!"

"I still want to be the flying monkey!"

(So much decision making. So much oral language.)

Four-year-old Toby tugged my arm, reminding me, "We're going to do the W. of O., right?"

Then Toby confided to our guest parents, "She'll only do it if we ask for it!"

That particular day, Tammie wanted us to explore the wonder of caterpillars turning into butterflies.

But first things first: tornado, house falling, Munchkins marching, characters meeting, Y.B.R., monkeys flying, witch melting.

Following those rituals, I suggested, "When Dorothy and her friends were traveling on the Y.B.R., they saw something in the grass along the way. Tiny, fuzzy, colorful little—hmmm—what kind of creatures could they be?" Easy to guess. We shook out of the W. of O. characters and turned ourselves into caterpillars crawling along, munching on leaves and plants. Talking and slowly changing, we evolved miraculously into beautiful butterflies and flew happily out of the room to the music of (surprise) "We're off to see the wizard..."

The children were happy. Tammie and Greg were happy.

When the children flew out of the room, one of the visiting dads turned to me with deadly serious eyes.

"If you're tired of the Wizard of Oz, why don't you just tell them no?"

I burst into almost uncontrollable laughter. Not once, never in all these weeks and months, had the thought occurred to me. *I could have said no!*

How could we say no when the children told us that they wanted to stay in Oz, that they could learn everything they needed to in Oz, that Oz had room in it for all skills, lessons, themes, concepts?

How could I explain to our guest that I was able to use the Wizard of Oz, which was where the children were, to connect them to where the curriculum wanted them to be?

How could we say no when the children told us that they wanted to stay in Oz, that they could learn everything they needed to in Oz, that Oz (and any other place or idea that intrigued them) had room in it for all skills, lessons, themes, concepts?

At the end of the year, the parents presented me with a gift. I am wearing it now, as I write this memory. It's a Wizard of Oz watch. Whenever I think that I, the teacher, am totally in charge of the children's learning, whenever I think that the children have no input into what inspires and fascinates them, I press the button on my watch and it plays, "Somewhere Over the Rainbow." My watch reminds me that there is no limit on the ideas children choose to love and no limit on what those ideas can encompass. They can encompass *everything!*

If you don't believe me, I'll send you a one-way ticket to the Emerald City with a watch that plays "Somewhere Over the Rainbow."

Just say *yes.*

Snowball

I am just bursting to tell you about the puppet in my life, Snowball, a little brown-and-white, floppy-eared puppy puppet. Eighteen years ago, the white part of his fur was brilliant white. It now borders on beige!

Snowball has an accumulation of eighteen years of children's germs, tears, fingerprints, sniffles, dribbles, whispers, clutches, hugs, tugs, and kisses on him. If you touch him, you will be immune to whatever bug is going around. When he retires (which is not in the foreseeable future), I will donate him to the National Institute of Health so they can use him for research on immunization. I'm sure he carries the cures to most of our dread diseases on his furry little paws, ears, and nose.

Snowball does not talk out loud. If he did, he would sound like he was from the Bronx, as I do, and the children do not need two New York City accents in their delicate Midwestern ears. Snowball whispers to me and I tell the children what he says. His communication with them may be nonverbal, but it is crystal clear.

Over the years,

- lonely children who never talked to anyone talked to Snowball.
- children who needed special cheering, TLC, reassurance, and comfort received those gifts in abundance from Snowball.
- unfriendly, troubled children stopped their aggressive behavior immediately when Snowball let them know that their negative actions hurt his feelings.
- children who were rarely noticed by their peers were always noticed by Snowball.

Thousands of children (including folks who were once children) can list more reasons for loving Snowball than did Elizabeth Barrett Browning when she wrote of her love for Robert. As time and space are limited (aren't they always?) I will give you a smattering of children's accolades for their special little friend:

- "He's such a good listener."
- "He's cute!"
- "He always cares about us and likes to be with us."
- "Even though he makes hundreds of mistakes,

he keeps trying and he's not ashamed if he goofs up."

- "He never, never leaves anyone out. If some-one feels sick or sad, he has extra kisses and hugs and makes them feel better."
- "He's sad when we're sad."
- "He's cuddly."
- "He's funny."
- "He's lovable."
- "We tell him secrets."
- "He does good tricks, like, 'if you're happy and you know it waggle your ears.' He's so silly."
- "If someone's mad he makes them laugh."
- "He's extra nice to new kids so they don't feel shy."

In our creative movement sessions with children, Snowball's participation is minimal in time but maximal (is this a word? I like it) in quality. He only shows up during the last few minutes of our classes, sending the children off with good-bye kisses.

Once we had a three-and-a-half-year-old boy, Jim, who was (and is) deaf. For weeks, he sat and watched our stories and dances but did not partici-pate. One day when Snowball was kissing the kids good-bye, Jim beckoned to me from his spot on the

sidelines, gesturing that Snowball had forgotten to
kiss one of the children. I thanked Jim and quickly
remedied the situation. At that
time, and to this day,
Snowball was called on to
do his favorite trick, the
peek-a-boo trick, which
he never got right. We
always showed
Snowball how to do it—
by covering up our faces
with our hands and repeating
the chant, "Where are the kids?"
three times before we revealed our
peek-a-boo faces. Ta da! But Snowball,
the slow learner, just couldn't get it.
(And he still can't.) We kept coaching him
to keep his furry little face hidden behind his
furry little paws while we chanted three times,
"Where's Snowball?" but he always popped out on
the count of one. This quirk kept the children in
gales of laughter. I would say, "Shall we give him
another chance?" Once a child giggled, "Let's give
him a million chances!"

Well, back to our friend Jim, who had never
uttered a single sound in his almost four years of living. His regular sessions at speech therapy were to
no avail. No one had ever heard his voice. Can you

Early childhood professionals are grossly underpaid, but they are real pros. For example, they try not to cry in front of the children.

guess what Jim's first spoken words were? You guessed it! "Where's Snowball?"

Early childhood professionals are grossly underpaid, but they are real pros. For example, they try not to cry in front of the children. That unforgettable day, we waited until the children departed for home before we permitted our tears to flow.

Snowball has been invited to more parties, sleepovers, suppers, picnics, trips, and holiday get-togethers than most humans on the planet. Recently, one of our early childhood classes was making cookies. As I watched the children mixing the dough, taking turns shaking in the sugar and sprinkling in the flavor, I felt a tug at my sleeve. Ezra, a strong, muscular boy, had a great idea. "Mim, why don't you go and get Snowball so he can join us for cookies?"

Snowball's magic is not limited to young children. Some years ago, I taught one of those total immersion weekend in-service courses for teachers, called, "More Fun Than a Field Trip: Teaching in the Key of Life." Snowball and I welcomed the participants at the doorway as they entered. Most of them smiled or waved to Snowball as they came in and found their seats. One gentleman arrived with a puzzled, hesitant expression on his face and a reluctant rhythm in his walk. He was a high school athletic coach and science teacher. When Snowball waved to him in greeting, the burly coach took a giant step back and threw me a disgusted, skeptical look. I knew he was thinking, "What the heck did I sign up for?"

We had to give him an A for effort. He stuck with our often off-the-wall antics for fifteen solid hours! At the close of the course, people departed with warm farewells and new friendships. Our tough high school coach/science teacher paused at the doorway, patted Snowball on the head, and said, "Bye, buddy!"

Summers, when my husband and I relax at the community center swimming pool, children of all ages ask, "Where's Snowball?" When I walk through shopping malls, arts festivals, pow-wows, and air- port terminals, children (and alumni who were once children) stop me and ask, "How's Snowball?"

Funny how a little brown-and-white (beige), worn but warm puppy puppet can be so memorable to so many people. Maybe we need Snowball to remind us that our children are longing for friends (human, ani- mal, puppet) who

- are good listeners
- never leave anyone out
- make them laugh
- cheer them on

- always have extra kisses and hugs to make them feel better when they're sick or sad
- can be trusted
- and love them (no matter what)

I learned a lot from Snowball!

The Whole Truth about Hole Language

Can You Dig It?

In my manic zigzags across the country, being with teachers, parents, and children, the most memorable moments are not those I spend giving keynote speeches or presenting workshops but those I spend with teachers and children hanging out and talking off the record about what's on our minds and in our hearts. During these last few years, one of the hottest topics among teachers has been whole language. I have heard the whole gamut of opinions and concerns, from total harmony with the Gestalt philosophy of whole language to nervous questions ("Is *this* whole language? Am I doing it right?") to challenges ("I don't get it! I thought I *was* doing whole language every Thursday. Look, here are my whole language dittos. *What does whole language mean anyway?*").

In my more frivolous mind-sets, I have thought that the quest for the definitive explanation of whole language is like the perennial search for signs of spring. It's important to encourage and reassure skeptics by showing them evidence of whole language in action. They need numerous examples. We need to demonstrate that whole language is not about descriptions on the printed page. It flourishes in the rhythm of everyday life. Signs of whole language in action are everywhere! For example:

One fine October day, during a break in a conference in beautiful Arcata, California, Pam Goldsmith, the director of Mad River Children's Center, invited me to visit her program. I was delighted. Snooping through her cheery, colorful rooms, which were rich with developmentally appropriate materials, resources, projects, and activities, I noticed something missing.

"Pam, where are the kids?"

Mumbling, "Oh-well-c'mon, we'll go see," Pam led me to the backyard. Walking out the center's back door, I couldn't help seeing the immensity of The Hole. Pam recited its statistics: 8 feet wide by 20 feet long and 3 feet deep! From deep in the hole came the voices of children laughing, playing, singing, counting. As we walked nearer, the scene grew clearer. Shoveling, probing, scooping dirt, and smoothing pathways, the children gleefully shouted as they discovered or uncovered buried toys. They hardly looked up to notice the stranger (me) standing with their director.

I forced Pam to tell me the story of this amazing hole.

"Well," she began, "one of our grandparents offered us a 20-foot aluminum boat for the kids to play with. So we began digging a hole for the boat in our yard. Everybody—kids and teachers—brought shovels, and we dug and dug and dug for ten days!"

Those ten days of the original digging were joyful times. As the children dug, they talked about discovering buried treasures, dinosaur bones, and precious stones.

From the hole, we could hear the children singing, "Found a pebble, found a pebble…" to the tune of "Found a Peanut" as they held up a newly discovered treasure.

"My pebble is a fossil!"

"I found a pirate's ring!"

The children went back to their explorations, and Pam continued the story.

"Digging the hole would have been fun just in itself! The digging itself would have been the end result, and everyone would have been happy. But as you see, even with the hole completely dug, the children love nothing more than continuing to dig and shape it and play in it."

Those ten days of the original digging were joyful times. As the children dug, they talked about discovering buried treasures, dinosaur bones, and precious stones. They found little vials, sticks, twigs, pebbles, miscellaneous (scrapped?) materials. They sang familiar and improvised songs. ("Found a Peanut" was their favorite.) They had counting races: Who could dig the most? The fastest? How many shovels did it take to fill the buckets? They experimented with every variety of digging arrangements: partners, small groups, and individuals. They read poems and stories about holes and dirt and dump trucks and building. Their favorite book was *Roxaboxen*.

After those ten glorious days, the hole was dug to the specifications. But the children found a bonus. Not only did they have a new beautiful, huge hole, but they had created a *mountain* of dirt!

"Believe it or not," Pam said, "no one cared about anything else but the hole. Every single child, everybody, all day, every day, lived in, on, and around the hole. We were thinking of changing our name to Mad River Children's Hole! Even the kindergarten kids ate snacks and lunches in the hole, on the mountain above the hole, or sitting around the hole!"

As Pam's narrative went on, the children began playing another game, "Rescue!" They slid a plank

into the hole and used it as a ramp, driving their toy
cars, trucks, and buses up and down it.

"Good thing you're helping..."

"It's a avalanche! Send a truck!"

"Help is coming. Here I come!"

As the rescue operation proceeded with
admirable efficiency and cooperation, Pam talked
about the rain.

"Well, later the rains came and water collected in
the hole. One day, we came to school and saw that
the water had frozen in the bottom."

Pam invited the kids to "check this out."

She broke off a chunk of ice so the children could
see that it was solid. They examined the ice and
dropped toys, rocks, branches, and boxes into the
hole to see which objects were heavy enough to
break the ice and which skidded across it. During
the following days, they watched frozen water melt,
making continuous observations, such as, "Last
night it wasn't as cold as before," and, "It got warm
out, and the big piece of ice got smaller."

When the bottom of the hole was filled with mud,
the hole became a dinosaur tar pit, the floor of the
sea, and mud-sliding hills. One day, the kids rolled all
the tricycles (about eight) down into the hole. They
had to really work together to get them all out,
cleaned up, and back in their places before the end

of the day. The project called for responsibility, hard work, and cooperation. Problem solving became an everyday, all-the-time activity. The day the tricycles were in the hole, some kids built a ramp with plywood to ease their journey up and out.

"They really got inventive!" Pam added with a twinkle of admiration.

One day one of the kids suggested, "Let's all hold hands and see if we can reach all the way around the hole." The Mad River children and teachers held hands, encircled the hole, walked together in one direction, reversed, walked-skipped-hopped the other way, and made, as Pam described, "our own little hole dance and song!"

Using pieces of plastic rain gutter, the children built bridges across the hole, pushing their toy vehicles along as they played, talked, planned, and sang. They constantly brainstormed:

"What if we moved the bridge here?"

"Try it."

"Let's build it here."

The older, after-school, K–3 kids knew they were on holy ground, and they wanted in. They turned themselves into architects and designed and built little cities and towns inside the hole, using mud shapes, blocks, rocks, PVC pipes, charms, and toys. They ran and jumped around the hole, singing mountain songs, railroad songs, traveling songs.

At one point, a few parents asked whether the hole was dangerous. Carefully evaluating every hole-centered activity (and that included virtually everything the children did—of course, under close supervision) the staff decided that the most danger-ous aspect was that everyone got totally muddy. The solution: extra clothing for every child and a bag each day for carrying the muddy clothes home!

The hole at Mad River Children's Center intrigued me. I wondered about it for weeks. For months. In January, almost four months after my visit to Arcata, I called Pam and asked for an update. You know, young children are supposed to have short attention spans and, heaven knows, these kids had already broken all records with their unrelenting fascination, so I expected Pam to tell me that the children were on a new interest and off the hole.

However, Pam cheerfully informed me, "The hole is still the center of everything! We had some bad weather and spent lots of time indoors. Even when we were inside, the talk and activities were about the hole! The kids looked out the windows at the rain and wondered how deep the water was. Would the mountain wash away? Would the yard be like a beach? Would our footsteps still show? Would our village be splattered with mud? Would we find our forgotten toys buried at the bottom of the rain-soaked hole?"

The older children spent the long indoor days drawing intricate plans and maps for their cities in the hole. The younger kids drew their own versions of maps. Now the walls of the rooms were covered with the children's designs, sketches, and maps of their hole and mountain.

People say if you dig deep enough, you'll reach China. Well, the Mad River hole bored deep enough into my imagination to inspire another transcontinental phone call to Pam some weeks later.

"What's happening?"

Five months after the digging of the hole, a natural disaster occurred. During one of the California storms, a big tree fell across the yard and covered the hole. Because the area had so much storm damage, the tree people had not yet arrived to cut up and haul away the huge tree.

"Guess what is now the center of our center?" Pam challenged. Before I could answer, she announced, "The tree!"

Pam's kids love their tree. They build on it and in it. They climb it, sketch it, and write about it in their journals, next to their hole sketches, poems, and notes. Singing it, dancing about it, they turn it into magic, into mystery, into trolls' bridges, animal shelters, homes for insects, and nests.

Pam's voice lowered as my phone bill grew. She confided, "Here's our problem. The grandpa with the boat asked Ken Freed, our assistant director, to look at the boat. (Remember the boat from last October?) Ken loves the boat and now has spent hours asking different companies to donate their services to pull it the ten miles to the center. He's organizing a Saturday for parents to volunteer to paint, sand, and ready the boat for the children. Of course, the boat has to wait for the tree to get out of the hole!"

Pam was trying to stall the boat, distract Ken. Forget the boat!

"See, when the tree is removed, the children will rediscover their hole, with all its enchantment, its exciting contents that they've forgotten about. I know they'll begin again with their love affair with the hole!"

She pondered, "If the boat finally arrives and settles into the hole, we'll just have to dig another hole!"

Black Elk, the great Oglala Sioux medicine man, said, "Anywhere is the center of the world." The children at the Mad River Children's Center have demonstrated for months that a simple hole in the ground can be the center of the world!

> Black Elk, the great Oglala Sioux medicine man, said, "Anywhere is the center of the world." The children have demonstrated for months that a simple hole in the ground can be the center of the world!

Stories and poems about holes and earth! Songs and dances! Maps, sketches, blueprints! Journal pages! Chants and plants! Brainstorming! Scientific observations! Wonderment and explorations! Conversations and cooperation! Connections! Imaginative play! Hands-on, interactive, multilayered, direct experiences! Projects and programs! Questions and problem solving! Counting and measuring! Geology, archaeology, physics! Predictions, comparisons, and conclusions! Physical fitness!

Pam's provocative words still ring in my ears: "If everything had gone in logical, predictable [boring?] sequence, imagine the immense learning that would have been missed."

I offer the hole in the backyard at Mad River Children's Center in Arcata, California, as a wholly delightful, holistic, wholesome example of whole language in action. Can you dig it?

Get the Elephant Out of the Room

We're finished with the E's!

Shiggy started it all when he wore his new fire-fighter's hat to our first movement session way back in September. He and his toddler colleagues came zooming into the dance room all fired up about fires. It was such a hot subject! How could I fight such enthusiasm?

Scrapping my plan to celebrate the folk tune "Old MacDonald Had a Farm" with music, dance, improvisation, animal dialogue, humor, and drama, I switched to the teacher version of automatic pilot (in other words, winging it) and created a story about firefighters:

"Once upon a time the firefighters were sleeping in the firehouse." (The children dropped to the floor, closed their eyes, and snored. Debbie, their good-sport teacher, tiptoed to the corner of the room. At my signal, she burst into arm-waving, finger-vibrating, torso-swaying flames. I sounded the alarm.)

"The firefighters jumped up, dressed quickly, slid down the pole, and hurried to their fire trucks!" (The children accompanied the narrative with rapidly changing movement patterns, demonstrating dressing, sliding, rushing.)

"Sirens blaring, the fire trucks raced around the city to the fire." (We always practice moving around the room in the same direction. This safety habit is deeply instilled in all the children of our school. On this day, the fire trucks raced around the city to the bouncy beats of exciting Israeli/Arab music. Because we always have the music of the world at our fingertips, we play the music of the world with all new ideas.)

"The firefighters arrived at the fire. They *uncurled* their hoses, *stretched* their ladders, *climbed up,* and *balanced* themselves as they *aimed* their heavy power hoses toward the flames. Finally, the fire was out!" (The fiery Debbie slowly drooped to the floor. High fives! Good job! To the percussive rhythms of African drums and bells, the fire engines raced back to the firehouse.)

Before I could steer us on to Old MacDonald's farm, as I had planned, the children sang out, "Can we do that again? Can we have another fire?" (Confession: I am a person who lets kids boss her around—especially when they are totally enthralled with an idea. I call the ideas children are madly in love with magic vocabulary. Obviously, *fire* headed Shiggy's classmates' "magic vocabulary" list.)

That first day back in September, we extinguished three major fires. One of them happened on Old MacDonald's farm! Debbie got triple aerobics points as she flared and flamed in different locations around the room.

"Is this in my job description?" she joked. "I'm almost burnt out!"

From that day on, Shiggy and his classmates continued rushing into every single movement session with their zealous chant, "Can we do the fire story?"

I never, ever mentioned the word *fire.* Yet the firefighters' story was always requested by the children in Shiggy's class. Whoever said that young children have short attention spans needs to visit a group of young children when they're immersed in a fascinating subject.

Confronted by this weekly challenge, I realized that my choices were limited to three:

Burn all my plans and curriculum guides.

Sweetly say, "Enough is enough already with the fires! We need to get on with our other very important work!"

Be creative, be imaginative, be flexible, be open
minded, be playful, be holistic, be courageous, be
tuned into the kids, be brilliant, and figure out ways
to link a fire to every other subject or topic. In other
words, make connections!

Naturally, I chose number three, over and over
again. Now it's months later, and I can report that
Shiggy's class has not missed a chance to work with
a fire story. We've integrated fires and firefighters in
every session. We've put out fires

- on Old MacDonald's farm
- on the Yellow Brick Road (didn't poor Scarecrow almost catch fire?)
- at the circus (all those torches and fireworks)
- on the property of the Three Pigs (remember
  when the wolf slid down the chimney into a
  pot of boiling water and burned his tush?)
- in the rain forest (forest fires are very
  dangerous)
- on the road with Jack Be Nimble (better jump
  very high over that candle stick, Jack!)

Have I made the point, or are more examples
necessary?

Despite all their textbooks and notebooks packed
with information, despite the research and scholar-
ship available to them, teachers and education students are always astonished at the daily situations
that their courses of study didn't cover—situations

that demand a combination of spontaneity, flexibility, imagination, boldness, instinct, faith, playfulness, and pure nerve to guarantee intelligent and loving responses.

I am relentless when presenting the alternatives: "Either you're open or closed! Either you're flexible or uptight! Either you're integrated or compartmentalized! Which side are you on?'

Over the last four-plus decades, I have experienced hundreds of incidents in which super-structured, inflexible teachers slammed shut doors that would have led to opportunities for joyful learning. They have said:

"It's not in my lesson plan."

"I didn't have enough advance notice."

"It doesn't fit into our schedule."

"It's not included in our curriculum."

"We've already finished fires."

But education is a dynamic, exciting, elusive, and mysterious process. Aren't the moments we remember most clearly, precisely the ones that simply *happened,* like Shiggy's firefighter story?

> Teachers and education students are always astonished at the daily situations that their courses of study didn't cover—situations that demand a combination of spontaneity, flexibility, and pure nerve to guarantee intelligent and loving responses.

Fire hats off to those creative teachers who put a marker in their daily plan books and embark with their children on adventures in uncharted territories! They design new combinations, discover amazing connections. The powerful elements of surprise, delight, appreciation, and comprehension dazzle the participants.

To such experiences, we bring everything that is in us as teachers—and even more. (Do we really know *all* of our gifts and resources?) The children contribute their best energy and ideas. Language flows and grows in these shared times when we are learning together on the journey.

This past February was a weird month. The temperature rose into the forties and fifties, ruining the kindergarten teacher's plan (marked "snow and snowpeople" in bold print). She always saves *snow* for what is usually the coldest month. She bases her worksheets, activities, and projects on bundling up and playing out in the snow. She could have been the kind of teacher who is rigid even when the month of February is not frigid! But she isn't. She could have said, "These are my well-prepared, carefully thought out plans. Even though the air is warm and there is no snow on the ground, we are going to follow these activities to the letter! They were good enough for the last ten Februaries, and they will be good enough for now. Business as usual!"

But she didn't. Instead, with a twinkle in her eye and a hang-loose sense of humor, she shared a new idea with her kindergartners. "How about if we put bikinis on our snowpeople?"

Giggling, the children celebrated snow figures and snow games, but the context and content were original. They listened to their teacher explain, "Boys and girls, if this was a regular, old-fashioned February, we would be surrounded by snow. Let's talk about snow!" And they did. They talked about statistics and weather records and average temperatures. They discussed comparisons, expectations, and patterns. They learned something of graphs and weather reports and predictions.

And the children enjoyed the planned activities and the fun-filled changes that enriched their awareness of how unusual the weather patterns of this particular month were. Their playful pictures expressed the new combinations.

Serendipity plays a huge part in the creative process. How do we seize the unexpected opportunities presented to us? Teachers who do not teach in the key of life have told me:

"Oh, we didn't have to see the convention on TV because we already finished government."

"We don't need to look for comets because we're not up to our space unit yet."

"When Sean brought in the small totem his grandmother carried for him from Alaska, I told him he had to wait his turn for 'show-and-tell.' And he wasn't scheduled for another week. Besides, we don't really study Alaska this year."

At an in-service workshop I presented, "Teaching in the Key of Life," many beginning and experienced teachers expressed concern about handling spontaneous, serendipitous challenges. (It's easier to simply dismiss the opportunities presented!)

I made up a story about a circus animal handler walking an elephant into a nearby elementary school. The two stood in the doorway of a classroom waiting for the teacher to invite them in.

"Pardon me," the teacher told the animal handler politely, "could you please get the elephant out of my room; we're finished with the letter E!"

From A to Z, we brainstormed ways to welcome the elephant!

Uh-oh, here comes Shiggy's class! Today's plan is to have a big Presidents' Day celebration. No doubt the fire department will lend us a few fire engines and firefighters to lead the festivities. What's a parade without a fleet of fire trucks? We never know when that fire alarm will go off, do we?

Telling
Time

Hurrying through the halls to the kindergarten room for my next Artists-in-the-Schools session, I heard calypso rhythms wafting through the closed door of the classroom I was looking for. I knocked, but no one answered, so I just went in.

"Day-O!" Pulsing steel drums and the bouncy lyrics of the "Banana Boat Song" filled the air as swaying children glided and danced around the room, singing along, twirling and stepping, smiling and improvising. I set down my own records, tambourine, and puppet, and joined their dance. When the song was over, we clapped and hugged. Shining faces greeted me. I looked around for the teacher and spotted her still sitting at her desk, putting papers away. I grinned at her.

"Such fun. What's going on?"

"Oh, we're just killing time," she answered.

Old trooper that I am, I plunged right into my
hour with the kindergartners. Still soaring and
delighted from the joy of the "Banana Boat Song," we
continued moving, singing, playing, dancing, and
telling stories. But something was chipping away at
the happiness I felt from being with the children. The
words *killing time* gnawed at my spirit.

If we could interview each and every child in that
class, I would bet my life that every one of them
would say that the best part of the day, perhaps the
best part of the school year thus far, was that short
precious period of singing and dancing together. Yet,
without malice or hurtful intentions and without
conscious negativism, their teacher described the
activity as "killing time."

In those few minutes, so much happened and so
many skills were called on: total participation and
cooperation, freedom of expression, oral language,
reviewing information (the lyrics, which everyone
already knew), rhythm, small and gross motor skills,
listening skills, multicultural education, sequential
learning, patterning, verbal skills, respecting the
space of others, repetition, and—most important—
enjoyment.

Think for a moment about your own school experiences. Think about those few minutes before a
guest arrives at your classroom door, when you and
the children are exchanging ideas, anticipating,

wondering what the person will be like, wondering how the visit will go, suggesting questions to ask. Do you consider that to be killing time? Perhaps those moments are peak times.

Consider the song sung together in the few minutes before the bell rings for assembly; the anecdotes children share before daily morning exercises officially begin; the complicated hand-clap/rap/chant songs the children teach each other in the few minutes of free time between getting drinks and the math lesson; the drawing, writing, sharing, talking, and joking time after lunch on a rainy day when outside recess is called off. Killing time or peak time?

Here are some times to record in your journal and imprint on your memory:

- Pnina standing against the classroom wall, sun shining on her back, explaining, "I love my shadow."
- Len playing the "Hokey Pokey" on his "violin" in those few seconds before the story begins.
- Ben bringing in the bird's nest his grandpa found—even though it wasn't sharing day.
- Antonio calling his classmates to the window to see the rarely seen white squirrel, just as quiet time is over and reading groups begin. "It looks like a ghost squirrel," observes Dylan with wide wonder in his eyes.

- Callie and Chloe sitting at table 1 during that waiting time before attendance is called, counting the little stones Callie keeps in her jacket pocket.
- Kindergartners joyful together, dancing and swirling to the "Banana Boat Song" before the Artist-in-the-School arrives.

Killing time? Peak time? Prime time? Hallowed time? Sometimes those incidental, in-between, hang-loose, unstructured, spontaneous times together are our *best* times. Perhaps the children (and we) will remember those times longest and with the most fondness.

Right now, on this day-o, what time is it in *your* classroom? How do you tell *your* time?

Schools Children Run To

The kids in Carol and Linda's room are fascinated with knights, dragons, and castles. Today they are building a castle out of blocks and scrounge materials.

"It won't be like a sand castle," one of the builders explains. "Tomorrow it will still be here!"

These pre-kindergarten children come from a variety of cultures, races, and religions. The animals in their room are a diverse family of classroom pets, from geckos, turtles, frogs, and fish to hedgehogs, chinchillas, snakes, and lovebirds (to name only a few). In Carol and Linda's room, the animals and children have a year-long love affair.

They meet in a brightly colored, improvised basement classroom (the building was not prepared for the overflow of infants, toddlers, and young children), which features numerous projects, excellent children's books, "our own art gallery," mobiles, sculptures, birds' nests, and well-used art supplies.

Almost-five-year-old Carly proudly shows me her "Carly's Book of Beautiful Planting."

Nature, the environment, animals, seasons, and community events are some of the major areas of interest and activity. Music, dancing, reading, playing, building, painting, observing and caring for animals, experimenting, and discovering are basic ingredients in the rich mix of magical moments that define daily life in this exciting place.

Children don't walk reluctantly or hesitantly to Carol and Linda's room. They run! They can't wait for the day to begin, for the adventure of the day!

Children don't walk reluctantly or hesitantly to Carol and Linda's room. *They run!* They can't wait for the day to begin, for the adventure of the day! Each morning, they know they will be greeted by loving and enthusiastic teachers. Today they know that their castle will be waiting for them. The water won't wash it away.

A few miles away, at a nearby school, all the kindergarten classes and one kindergarten–first grade combination class have caught the contagious theme of (what else?) dinosaurs. As this school offers a program of informal education enriched by a valued arts team, which works in close collaboration with the classroom teachers, each kindergarten class designs its own unique medley of explorations and information gathering. Few worksheets or dittos in this school!

In this warm climate of continuous sharing, first grader Karl brings in his favorite book, *The Dinosaur Stomp*. Everyone loved its wacky story about dinosaurs getting ready for their big dance, called a stomp! When Karl carries the book into Marlene's dance class, she catches the children's enjoyment and runs with it. After all, the dinosaurs are getting ready to party! Expanding on the story, the children and Marlene learn dances from around the world. Multiplying ideas, working cooperatively, making decisions, the children combine their own movement patterns with the story of dinosaurs, with dinosaurs' timelines through history, with their stomp party! Soon *all* the kindergarten classes are in on the fun and are busy planning their sharing for families and community. The kids are so excited that many of them even teach their families the dances!

The children are afraid to get sick! How could they miss a single day? On the evening of the sharing, the children and their families don't walk to school. They stomp! They dance! They *run* to school!

Don't take my word for it. Observe young children on their way to school, to child care programs, to home care. Their feet barely touch the ground as they bound eagerly through the open doors. They can't wait to start the day. Even if they feel under the weather—sniffly, tummy-achy, itchy—they insist on not missing! The climate and the teachers in their programs, in their schools, have healing powers.

No matter what the building's structure, or the age of its materials, these special places are filled with love, welcome, surprises, laughter, interesting and inviting experiences, and activities that promise challenge, delight, and success. The children know they will be safe at any speed.

Intensive themes, such as the dinosaurs I have described, are not necessary for capturing the spirit of children. Sometimes the simplest things are the best. A teacher paints a large ice cream container, cuts a small hole in it, and turns it into a mouse house. Every day, she reaches into the mouse house and finds—ta tum—a few letters from the mouse to different children.

Early one still-dark morning, a family hears sounds downstairs. Nervously, the parents tiptoe down, expecting to confront an intruder, only to find their kindergartner dressed and ready for school— two hours early!

"What are you doing up so soon?" they ask, astonished.

"I've got to get to school early today!" Their child jumps with impatience. "I think I have a letter from the mouse!"

Is today the day the children will wrap bean seeds in moist paper towels, place them in plastic sandwich bags, and tuck them cozily into their pockets to make pocket gardens? Or is today the day they will see their bean seeds sprout with their very own eyes?

Is today the day when they make drums out of coffee cans and cereal containers or is today the day when their puppets will tell a story?

Hang out with the children. Play with them. Talk to them. Listen to them. Kids tell us and show us how they want to be taught. Are we listening?

You can bet that in classes like these, young children are learning in enriching, multidimensional, joyful, playful, open-ended ways. Their days are rich with interesting, diverse materials and a wide variety of experiences that help them make connections, find meanings, make sense of the world. In such sacred places, children learn on many levels, through a combination of methods and materials: for children who love to work with their hands, clay, sand, wood, mud, sticks, and stones; for children who love to dress up, clothes for imaginative play; for music makers and movers, instruments and songs; for mathematicians and engineers, maps and numbers and board games.

Hang out with the children. Play with them. Talk to them. Listen to them. Kids tell us and show us how they want to be taught. Are we listening?

I'm impressed with programs that children run to.

But there is a flip side. Nowadays, with such an emphasis on academic achievement, on skills and drills and tests and benchmarks, the pressure is on to take the fun out of fundamentals. Observe joyless schools that repel their students. Watch downcast, reluctant kids on their way to dreary, stiff, scary, boring places. In such places, children come to school healthy and get sick.

Here, Big Books, sandboxes, housekeeping corners, and puppets have been removed from the kindergarten room. After all, how can we allow these young students to play around when they need to be prepared for the serious world of education? The teacher is showing them a chart of long vowel sounds and short vowel sounds. After a few minutes, one of the boys goes to the rest room. When he returns, he cheerfully announces, "I think I understand! I just had a long vowel movement!"

When we round up the fun, the adventures, the surprises, the celebrations of ideas, and the open-ended, active, and interactive components of the joy of learning, and then remove them from our children's daily experiences, we deserve long vowel movements!

No question about it: as a major national issue, early childhood education is it. Researchers add information on a regular basis. Educators and parents, politicians and community leaders, churn with dialogue and debate as they try to decide what and how young children should learn. Which way will we go with early childhood education? Will we enhance children's lives or diminish them? Will we entice the children, invite them, delight them with exciting, inspiring, memorable learning moments, hours, days? Or will we discourage them, bore them, frighten them, shrivel them? These are crucial choices. There's no neutrality when we're dealing with the strong but delicate spirit of our young children.

While the debates intensify and are all too often polarizing and political, the children have their own agendas, their own expectations. Fortunately, many will not be walking but will be running to school!

Carol Highfield and Linda Muzzo teach pre-kindergarten at the Leo Yassenoff Jewish Center's Early Childhood Program in Columbus, Ohio.

Marlene Robbins teaches dance; Karen Mughan, Emilie Pitzer, Shelly Reed, and Michelle Devoll teach kindergarten; Sharon Sazdanoff teaches music; Jim McMahon teaches art; and Tracy McCarty teaches kindergarten through first grade combination class at Indianola Alternative Elementary School in Columbus, Ohio.

What do we want our children to learn? I'm sure our wish list would include such noble goals as language development, comprehension, vocabulary recognition, listening skills, communication and cooperative learning skills, respect, multicultural understanding, verbal skills, imagination, creativity, literature appreciation, self-confidence, and self-esteem.

These important proficiencies are acquired through myriad methodologies and materials. In our too often test-driven time, with schedules growing tighter by the moment to make room for practicing for tests, scoring, and measuring, we may easily forget a time-tested, universally delightful and beloved way of learning—*stories!* Stories fit all ages, places, time frames, and circumstances. They can happen on a walk, in a car, in the water, in an airport, on a visit. They can even happen in a gym or a classroom! As we fall under the magical spell of stories, we check off items on our academic wish list! Those excellent outcomes are woven into the colorful patterns we continually create in the telling, the listening to, the celebration of stories.

Even before their seatbelts are buckled, before Noah (twenty-two months) gets strapped into his car seat and relaxes with his sippy cup of apple juice, before we pull out of the driveway to begin our hour's journey to Seaquarium, Len (six) and Dylan (four) insist:

"Tell us a story!"

Grandpa Howard checks directions on the map while I check out directions for their stories with the boys. It's always their story.

"True or made up?"

"Made up."

"Want to use your real names?"

"No. I'll be Michael," Dylan says.

"I'll be Nicholas," Len decides.

"What about Noah?"

"He can be Jeremy."

We settle in for the ride and I remember some very important facts:

Dylan is in love with superheroes. This week's favorites are Batman and Robin. Len is a sports maven who knows every player of every team of every major sport. No matter what our plot is, a heroic deed by Batman and Robin must occur. An exciting sports adventure is imperative. And I must keep in mind that the protagonists of this story are Michael, Nicholas, and Jeremy.

"Once upon a time," I begin, "these three guys, Michael, Jeremy, and Nicholas, went with their grandparents on a trip. Where do you think they were going?"

Five minutes of vigorous discussion about their destination. Finally, inspired by a recent rainy-day trip to the Museum of Discovery, where we enjoyed a simulated space ride to the moon, the boys decide on the Museum of Discovery.

"A strange thing happened while the boys were in line waiting their turn to go on the space ride to the moon."

I pause dramatically to check in for instructions.

"Shall we make it funny or scary or what?"

"Scary," says Nicholas.

"Funny," says Michael.

It will have to be a combination. As the plot thickens, the boys decide to change their names.

"I don't want to be Michael anymore," says Dylan. "I'll be Jordan."

"And, I'll be Peter," Nicholas/Len announces.

Fortunately, Jeremy/Noah is content to listen attentively, slurping away on his sippy cup and happy to be Jeremy.

As the miles and minutes speed by, the boys get closer to their turn to enter the moon ride chambers. They watch the people ahead of them as they disappear behind the sliding doors. They hear the blast-off noises—lights flash, engines roar, then silence. A few minutes later, the people emerge from their ride. Now it is Jordan, Peter, and Jeremy's turn. It's weird. When they get into the space cabin, no one else is with them. The doors close. Ten, nine, eight, seven, six, five, four, three, two, one, *blast-off!* Whoooa, the space cabin is *not* a ride in the museum. It's *real!* They're really and truly flying out into space!

"We need Batman and Robin!" Jordan trembles with excitement and grabs Peter's hand.

The boys fly through space and land on the moon.

"Scary? Funny? Strange? Mysterious? Silly? What do you want to happen?" I like to offer a wide range of options.

The story continues for the entire hour it takes to drive to Seaquarium. It's not quite over when we arrive and the boys postpone going inside to listen to the end of the story, where Batman helps them return to earth after a sensational moon landing that features a game between two champion moon teams. Len explains that it's hard to throw a ball with no gravity. Only then do we go inside.

Our Seaquarium day comes to a spectacular sunset ending. Len, Dylan, and Noah are belted back into the car for the trip home. Howard barely has time to turn the key in the ignition when the boys insist:

"Tell us a story!"

"Well," I say, "everyone's tired so let's make a long story short!"

"No!" Len corrects. "Let's make a short story long!" And we do—all the way home.

Chloe, who has just turned three, runs to greet us at the airport. Before we take the escalator down to the baggage claim, she puts in her request. "Tell me a story!"

"Shall we use your name?"

At three, we want our names to be in the center of all our stories.

"Yes. Tell it about Chloe."

"What do you want our story to be about?"

Chloe is into animals, dinosaurs, lost and found, and mean and nice.

I'm not surprised when she says, "A turtle."

"Once upon a time"—we begin walking toward the baggage area of the airport—"there was a very shy little turtle who always hid in her shell." We stop and crunch down, into our shells. Chloe hides her face. "I'm in my shell," she whispers from behind her hiding hands.

"Everyone was looking for the little turtle but couldn't find her. All they could see was a green turtle shell."

"Well," I say, "everyone's tired so let's make a long story short!" "No!" Len corrects. "Let's make a short story long!" And we do—all the way home.

While Chloe's mom and dad pick up the luggage, the little turtle stays hidden in her shell, waiting for a friendly person to find her.

"Finally, along came a very nice girl named— what do you think?"

"Chloe!"

"Right! Chloe came skipping along." The turtle emerges from her shell and turns into a skipping Chloe.

"Chloe sees the shy little turtle shell and says, 'C'mon out, little turtle. Don't be afraid. I won't hurt you. You can come home and live with us!'"

Chloe peeks from behind her hands. A shy smile warms her turtle face.

"And they lived happily ever after."

Before Chloe stops clapping for that story, she is already requesting another. And another and another. We tell stories about the mean dragon who turned nice and the mean girl who turned nice but mostly about the shy turtle who found a friend named Chloe.

Finally, I suggest, "It's your turn, honey. How about telling Grandma Mimi a story?"

In her most dramatic storytelling voice, she says:

"Once upon a time. The end!"

Ryan (two) must have a horse in every story. Big sister Callie (five) loves stories about friends, family, activities, animals, fairies, princesses, elves.

As we burst into the house for our visit, we are greeted by two children chanting, "A story! A story!"

We sit on the floor and tell our stories. Ryan decides on the color of his horse: black.

We clap a galloping rhythm, slap our thighs, thump the floor, "Giddyap! Giddyap!"

"Once upon a time, this beautiful horse was galloping through the woods."

"The enchanted woods," corrects Callie.

"Of course, the enchanted woods. The horse is singing a beautiful horse song. Can you sing it?"

"I'm a beautiful horse, ho, ho, ho, a beautiful horse, ho, ho, ho," Callie sings.

"Ho, ho, ho," joins in Ryan, so happy to have a story that begins with a horse.

"The horse could be looking for a princess to ride him," Callie suggests.

"Great idea! The beautiful horse had no princess to ride him. He looked everywhere for a princess and finally…"

"He found her sleeping in the forest."

Callie and I go on with the story, with sparks of "ho, ho" from Ryan, along with galloping handclaps to accompany the search.

When the horse finally finds the sleeping princess, she wakes up and jumps on him and they gallop away together. Callie jumps up, runs to her crayons and markers and announces, "We better do some pictures about this story—Ryan, want to make a horse?"

"Stories need pictures!" Callie proclaims as she begins her illustrations.

Five-year-old Marissa loves the stories her grand-mother, Sarah (whom Marissa calls Bimi), tells her. One day, they were riding along discussing a recent news story about a car that fell into a hole. Oh, it was a big discussion! They wondered how it would feel to fall into a hole. Suddenly, Marissa turned to her grandmother and said, "I want to tell you a story, Bimi."

Sarah was thrilled. Marissa started her story,

"Well, there was this little girl who fell into a hole that went into another hole that went into a cave. She found a red flower and picked it. She came back with the flower. Everyone wanted it. She gave it away. So she went back to the cave to get another flower but a rock was in front of it and she couldn't get in. So everyone had to figure out how to grow their own flowers."

Sarah exclaimed, "Oh, Marissa. It's so nice to have you tell me a story!"

"Bimi, does that remind you of when you were a little girl and someone told you a story?"

"It sure does—where did you get that story?"

"I believe everything with my imagination!" Marissa said.

Treading water for a half an hour while my skin puckers and my toes begin to grow webbing, I eavesdrop on five children playing Little Mermaid on the other side of the pool. They talk nonstop about who's playing what character, what each one says, what comes next in the story.

"I'm Ariel and you be Ursula."

"I don't want to be Ursula."

"You can't sing when your tongue is cut out, no more."

"I want to be Ariel's father."

I am mesmerized as I listen and watch the children splash, jump, dive, dialogue, sing, and argue the story. This is the third day they have played Little Mermaid in the pool. They saw the movie three days ago.

They are still deep into the story when their mother calls them out for supper.

"But I can't walk yet. I have no legs," the Little Mermaid protests.

"I'll carry you, Ariel," the mom says, wrapping the Little Mermaid in a tie-dye beach towel.

The third graders are prancing, jogging, leaping, skipping around the gym, warming up for our story.

"Once upon a time," I begin, "this kid was out in the beautiful woods on a gorgeous day like today. So much energy! What could that kid be doing?"

Ideas always come fast and furiously.

"Running."

"Skipping."

"Bouncing a ball."

"Dancing."

We choreograph all the suggestions and arrange them in a sequence. Today I play rhythmical percussion music from the Middle East as the children run, jump rope, skip, pick flowers, dance, and bounce balls in creative movement around the gym.

I always ask the students to make choices, so I shout, "Everyone choose your favorite part and dance it!"

Twenty-six different ideas and patterns. We change to another favorite and celebrate it. What a beautiful day in the woods!

We rest. We catch our breath. I continue with the story:

"Well, after so much energetic activity, that kid was exhausted. Whew! And hungry too. But, no fast food restaurant or picnic table in sight. Nothing to eat and nowhere to rest, but—wait, what's that across the field in the woods? A little house."

I tap a knocking rhythm on my tambourine.

"Let's knock on the door. No one home. Let's try again."

Tap. Tap. Tap.

"Let's turn the doorknob to see if anyone is home."

We all twist our wrists and hands to find...

"Uh oh! No one is home, but the door is open! Shall we go inside?"

We walk together to a steady tambourine beat.

"There, on a table, the kid sees three bowls of porridge—a big bowl, a middle-sized bowl, and a little bowl."

The story is interrupted by a third grader who bursts with the discovery:

"Oh my God! It's Goldilocks!"

And so it is. Laughing, dancing, chanting, we go on with the story. Surprise!

Folktales from around the world are the focus of the fifth graders. Today, we will play with the story of Ananci and the story box. Through music, drama, dance, and dialogue, followed by visual arts and creative writing, we freely adapt the story. The marvelous African rhythms of Montego Joe accompany our dance/drama as everyone dances all the characters, all the actions of the story.

We dance the proud, powerful Sky God and the spider, Ananci, spinning a web from earth to sky, then climbing up till he reaches the Sky God.

We dance the Sky God presenting his treasured story box, which contains all the stories in the world. We show how Ananci wants the story box, but the Sky God demands that he meet three challenges first:

"Bring me the leopard with the gleaming teeth, the stinging hornets, and the impossible-to-see little spirit ghost."

We dance Ananci climbing back to earth down his ladder web and searching for the leopard, the hornets, and the spirit ghost. As he catches each one of them, he dances with joy. Now up, up, up the ladder they climb, back to the Sky God. Yes, here they are! The leopard pounces across the sky. The buzzing hornets buzz. The elusive little spirit ghost sways and swirls, never keeping the same shape.

Ananci is presented with the story box, but he can't wait to open it so he lifts the cover and all—all—the stories of the world float down to earth, every single one of them, and they are floating still to this very day.

Ananci is presented with the story box, but he can't wait to open it so he lifts the cover and all—*all*—the stories of the world float down to earth, every single one of them, and they are floating still to this very day. Oops, I think a story just landed on your shoulder. Did you just step on a story? Look in your pocket, you might find a story hiding there!

The fifth graders walk home looking for stories, waiting for stories to find them, to land on them, to float down to them as they keep on the lookout.

The next day, every child comes to school with a story to tell, to write, to illustrate, to dance, to read, to sing, to recite, to sculpt, to share.

"Tell it again!" says Dylan.

"Make a short story long!" says Len.

"Stories need pictures!" says Callie.

"Ho, ho, ho," says Ryan.

"Oh my God! It's Goldilocks!" says Scott.

"I believe everything with my imagination!" says Marissa.

"Once upon a time. The end," says Chloe.

(What do *you* say? How do *you* celebrate stories?)

Whether we follow these stories while treading water or driving through holiday traffic, we can imagine the fascination, the excitement of the children in the experience of storytelling. Storytelling (unless it's reduced to a test question on a standardized exam) is a dynamic and creative process. Stories are told and retold, changed and rearranged. Vocabularies grow! Understanding of plot, character, conflict, and drama increases. The abilities to make comparisons, see relationships, and find connections expand. Are our stories true or made-up? Are they fiction or nonfiction? Can we predict their endings? Do they include chants, poems, refrains? Are they rhythmic? Are they full of mysteries? Stories as old as caves and as new as today all celebrate language, enriching imagination and wonder—our uniquely human gifts.

When we make room in our rooms, when we make time in our time for the sharing of stories, we help our students learn about the *story* in *history,* the adventures of journeys, the overcoming of obstacles, and the miracle of courage, faith, and wit. And as our children are welcomed by us (and we by them) into the enchantment of stories, they become more skilled at storytelling, their academic skills are strengthened, and their too often diminishing spirits are nourished.

A Letter to the Families and Friends

of the Children in Room 13

Thank you for responding to our call for scrounge items. When you come to the open house next week, you'll notice that our huge basket of stuff is almost empty! Look for remnants of it in our homemade instruments, inventions, puzzles, museum exhibits, collections, and constructions, and in our imaginative sculpture show in the gallery area. Amazing what our talented kindergarten artists and scholars created from your cereal boxes, egg crates, coffee cans, toilet paper and paper towel rolls, clear plastic boxes, and fast-food Styrofoam containers. Please keep these excellent materials coming in, as we have many more things to do with them, always. The children are becoming more aware of how often we just toss away such valuable materials, so our scrounge works help our environment.

Thanks for answering the survey letter we sent out during the first week of school, asking you to jot down any areas of your experience that you're willing to share with the children. We've already welcomed three honored guests and learned a lot from them:

- Adam's grandfather told us about his work as a school custodian. The children listened intently as he talked about all the things he has to do to keep a school running smoothly and safely. They asked some very thoughtful questions.
- Anthony's aunt taught the kids how to design and make lovely bead patterns and introduced them to braiding. Marvelous for small and gross motor skills. (And counting, colors, sorting.)
- Destiny's mom told us about her job working in the housewares department of a big department store. The children loved the catalogues she shared and were fascinated by all the different household items and appliances she had to know about.

Of course, all of our classroom guests received beautifully written and illustrated thank-you letters from each child.

Now, about Our Place. Some of you have expressed concern that the kindergartners in room 9 down the hall seem to be more focused on practicing basic skills than our children here in room 13.

You were impressed with their seatwork, paperwork, and structured lessons. We respect the different ways children are learning in our school, and we are eager to tell you about the developmentally appropriate practices approach we are sharing with your children in Our Place. We deeply believe that the students in room 13 are learning their basic skills, but in diverse ways, which we will try to describe and which you'll have the chance to see for yourselves at the open house next week (or at any time you care to visit us—you're always welcome.)

You may notice that our room is a bit cluttered! So much is happening here that sometimes it's impossible to get organized and neat (even for the open house).

Our dress-up center is very popular (thanks to you folks who sent in the clothing—the children *love* it). Our M. N. M. trio (Monte, Nicole, and Michele) are deeply into playing with their costumes first thing every morning. You can't imagine all the oral language, vocabulary, listening skills, and social development that grow with dress-up dramas!

You'll understand why we advocated for keeping our sandbox when you see how most of the children enjoy it. We think they must be the descendants of desert people! Especially Tiffany and Juan, who lead the group to the sand every free-activity time. Among their numerous projects are tunnels, cities, buried treasures (they love playing archaeologists), and sandscapes. Last week, Latia joined in and surprised everyone by writing the whole alphabet in sand. We called it "sandmanship." The children are learning so much about measuring—cups/pints/quarts/gallons—in their world of sand.

Be careful when you stop at the inventions lab. Lamar and Jennifer are deep at work on a very intricate invention-in-progress. We can't wait for them to introduce it and explain it to us. Remember, these scientific breakthroughs take time, so we have to be patient. A lot of problem solving, decision making, and cooperative learning go along with this invention. They promised to try to finish it in time for our science fair (which you will learn about soon).

Have the children told you about their fabulous musical instruments? They're constructed of and decorated with scrounge and found objects, in colorful and original ways. Every day we use our instruments for stories, parades, sound effects, math, science, special events. In our weather study, we composed a blustery thunderstorm symphony. On Tuesday, we enriched our math lesson by adding one instrument at a time until we listened to the sum of all the parts. Then we subtracted one after another until we had silence—zero. We like to compose rhythms using numbers and patterns. Of course, we can't help dancing to our wonderful music! You would too! (We often

write down our choreography. For example, 10
jumps/5 kicks/10 jumping claps/2 wiggle-wiggles/
repeat.) Easy to follow and so much fun to do. If we
have time, we'll demonstrate at the open house.

Our room is drenched in language! Words! Posters!
Signs! Charts! Cartoon labels! Letters! Our word wall is
packed with words the children suggest and recognize.
Doesn't it make great wallpaper? The class rules promi-
nently posted on the door were discussed and agreed
upon by the children. Our mailbox is bursting with
mail, which gets delivered every day. It takes time to
help the children write and read their letters. They love
to get mail! Notice the postage stamps they designed.
Their letter and word recognition and comprehension
are strengthened every day in everything we do.

The orange flip chart near the nature table is our
song book. Look through its large, bright pages.
Read the words to all the songs your children know.
Remember, the music teacher is on maternity leave,
but we sing every day anyway. The children recognize every song and follow the words as we sing. Is
this singing or reading? (We say it's both!) We love
the illustrations the children designed for each song.

Reading is happening all the time in Our Place.
We don't limit reading to one specific time slot.
We're almost finished with the Ananci stories. We
read a story or a poem every day after lunch. Our
nature-loving students are immersed in books about

butterflies, dinosaurs, fish, and volcanoes. All the children are fascinated by the variations of the Cinderella story told by people around the world. Even though the holidays are still far off, the children want to hear Michael Joel Rosen's *Elijah's Angel* over and over!

And our kids count! Numbers are everywhere in Our Place. We count days, months, colors, shoes, pockets, loose teeth, pebbles, clouds. We measure and graph everything! Right now, our birthday graph is very popular!

We mustn't forget to tell you about the turtle. One of our colleagues from a nearby school was driving along when she saw a huge turtle in the middle of the road. Thrilled to find such a serendipitous treasure, thinking of how her second graders would love to meet such an interesting animal, she jumped out of her car to pick it up. As she carefully set it in the back seat, she remembered that her school was committed to a very rigid, tightly scheduled, solidly structured curriculum with very little time for any diversion. Most of each day was spent preparing the children for testing, for practicing skills and drills in a school-wide teaching program. Reluctantly, she gave the turtle to us.

We can't begin to describe the countless ways our turtle has inspired rich and meaningful learning experiences! Check out the shelf of books about turtles that the children are reading. Their questions about turtles filled our wonder chart and started us off on research and adventures. You'll learn from their turtle books and charts about different kinds of turtles—like snapping turtles, painted turtles, box turtles. In the turtle log, next to the habitat they built, they've written very interesting observations. You'll see how their handwriting is growing clearer every day. Their vocabulary continually delights us. We've discovered many turtle legends and myths from different cultures. At the beginning of the year, we didn't know that the turtle is a very important animal and symbol in many traditions! Did you? Next week, at the open house, the children will present their own interpretation of the legend of Turtle Island, accompanied by original music, dialogue, chants, and dances. The costumes, props, and scenery were built from your scrounge materials. Soon you'll receive your invitation to the program made for you by your kindergartner.

Our newest classmate, Molly, who came from China last month, is learning more and more English each day, as all her class neighbors are excellent tutors and we do so much talking all the time. (How else to learn a language but to talk a lot?) Yesterday, on our field trip to a nearby field, all the children wanted to hold Molly's hand and be her helpers as we celebrated our senses and wrote and drew impressions of our field study in our sketch books.

When you come to the open house, you'll see our classroom helpers board, with jobs for every child every day. Many of the twenty-four jobs were suggested by the kids. It takes all of us working together to contribute to the success and happiness of our group.

Included in your open house packet next week will be a description of developmentally appropriate practices from the National Association for the Education of Young Children, as well as an informational sheet about the multiple intelligences. (We all learn through and from our own unique mix of strengths and interests.)

We're eager to welcome you and tell you how much we love your children and how happy we are to be with them in Our Place, room 13.

> Sincerely,
> The Teachers of the Children in Room 13

P.S. We've had a few instances when children were *really* sick (fever, etc.) but tried to hide their symptoms so they could come to school. The third-grade brother of one of our students explained that his sister was "playing healthy" so she wouldn't miss. We were flattered but are concerned about their well-being. Thank you.

Other Resources from Redleaf Press

**For the Love of Children: Daily Affirmations for People
Who Care for Children**
by Jean Steiner and Mary Steiner Whelan
An empowering book filled with quotes, stories, thoughts, and
affirmations for each day of the year.

**What the Kids Said Today: Using Classroom Conversations
to Become a Better Teacher**
by Daniel Gartrell
Use the conversations in your classroom to build skills in the
children you care for. Contains 145 stories from 60 staff members at Head Starts, centers, and kindergartens.

Help Yourself! Activities to Promote Safety and Self-Esteem
by Kate Ross
Help Yourself! contains fun and creative ways to use songs as a
springboard into a curriculum for promoting self-esteem and
safety skills among young children. Written for use with the CD
of the same name by Cathy Fink and Marcy Marxer.

More Infant and Toddler Experiences
by Fran Hast and Ann Hollyfield
This sequel to the popular *Infant and Toddler Experiences*
contains more than 100 engaging new ways to fill infants' and
toddlers' lives with rich experiences that reflect and celebrate
each child's development.

More Than Letters
by Sally Moomaw and Brenda Hieronymus
Filled with dozens of fun and engaging activities designed to
make literacy a meaningful adventure for children. Contains an
extensive whole-language curriculum that creates a print-rich
classroom environment.

Call toll-free 800-423-8309
www.redleafpress.org